Light & Easy
Chinese
With Quick Wok Cooking

PUBLICATIONS INTERNATIONAL, LTD.

ISBN: 1-56173-782-8

Recipe development by Karen A. Levin
Photography by Sacco Productions Limited/Chicago
Photographers: Laurie Proffitt and Peter Walters
Photo Stylist/Production: Betty Karslake
Food Stylists: Lois Hlavac and Carol Parik
Assistant Food Stylist: Moisette Sintov McNerney

Pictured on the front cover, clockwise from top right: Wonton Soup (*page 8*), Easy Wonton Chips
(*page 10*) and Beef Soup with Noodles (*page 10*).

Pictured on the back cover, from top to bottom: Shrimp Toast (*page 18*), Cellophane Noodle Salad
(*page 72*), Pepper Beef (*page 22*) and Almond Chicken (*page 42*).

8   7   6   5   4   3   2   1

Manufactured in U.S.A.

CONTENTS

EASY COOKING, CHINESE-STYLE

Chinese cooking, as we know it, is actually a combination of cooking techniques and seasonings from all the regions of China. Northern or Beijing cooking features wheat noodles, dumplings, sweet-sour sauces, garlic and green onions. The coastal areas around Shanghai are known for their fabulous seafood and delectable sauces. Szechuan and Hunan cooking use a blend of seasonings to create dishes that have a combination hot, sour, sweet, salty taste all in one bite. Southern or Cantonese cooking, which is mildly seasoned and frequently served in Chinese-American restaurants, emphasizes cooking with soy sauce, ginger and sherry. We have taken the best from these regions to create the delectable recipes in this book.

These recipes have been developed with the health-conscious cook in mind. While this is not a diet book, many of the recipes have been lightened by omitting fat-laden cooking techniques and reducing fat, cholesterol and calories. For example, deep-fat frying techniques are not included in the book; instead recipes are modified to be stir-fried, baked or pan-fried in a small amount of oil. Also, egg whites have been substituted for whole eggs whenever possible, and ground chicken and turkey are used in place of pork for some recipes.

These recipes were designed to be easy with no-fuss cooking techniques, clear step-by-step directions and readily available ingredients. Before you begin, read the recipe thoroughly. Then do any marinating, soaking and chopping before cooking. The final dish will be sure to be a hit!

Cooking Techniques

Although a variety of familiar cooking techniques are used in preparing Chinese dishes, stir-frying, the most popular technique, is featured throughout this book. Before you begin, take a few minutes to read the following information. Stir-frying is easily mastered, and these helpful guidelines will enhance your enjoyment of these wonderful dishes.

Stir-frying involves the rapid cooking of ingredients in a small amount of oil over medium-high to high heat for a few minutes. In addition to saving time, the quick cooking preserves the nutrients, flavors, textures and colors of the food. Stir-frying can be divided into two separate steps—preparing the ingredients and cooking the ingredients.

It is essential to have all the ingredients prepared in advance. This means all cleaning, cutting, measuring, combining, etc. Stir-frying proceeds so quickly that there is no time to do anything else once cooking begins. When cutting meats and vegetables, make the pieces a uniform shape and size to ensure even cooking. Otherwise, one ingredient may overcook, while others are undercooked.

When you're ready to begin, place a wok or large skillet over medium-high or high heat. Preheating the pan prevents the food from sticking. When a drop of water added to the pan sizzles, the pan is sufficiently hot. Next add the oil, swirling to coat the inside of the pan; heat until the oil is hot, about 30 seconds. Now the ingredients can be added.

Stir-fry the meat first and remove. Then add the vegetables, beginning with those that take the longest to cook. Briskly toss and stir with a flat metal or wooden spatula. Be sure to keep the food in constant motion. This ensures that all surfaces are quickly coated with hot oil to seal in the flavorings, and also prevents overcooking or burning. To maintain the characteristic Chinese tender-crisp quality, serve stir-fried dishes immediately.

The best oils to use for stir-frying are vegetable oils that can withstand intense heat without smoking. Peanut oil, corn oil and soybean oil are excellent choices.

Helpful Hints

• When removing stir-fried meat, poultry or seafood from the wok, always place the meat in a clean dish, not one that held the raw or marinated food.

• Any foods that need to be marinated over 20 minutes should be marinated in the refrigerator.

• Resealable heavy-duty plastic food storage bags are great to use for marinating foods.

• Always have all the ingredients prepared—sliced, measured, marinated, combined—before you begin stir-frying, and have them located close to the wok.

• Stir any cornstarch mixtures before adding them to the hot wok. The cornstarch needs to be dissolved in the liquid to prevent it from lumping.

• Partially freeze beef, pork or poultry to make it easier to slice into thin strips.

• For a no-fuss stir-fry, use vegetables, such as sliced mushrooms, broccoli or cauliflower florets, spinach or bean sprouts, from the deli bar of the supermarket or frozen mixed vegetables, such as a broccoli and cauliflower combination.

• Use fresh flour tortillas from the supermarket dairy case in place of mandarin pancakes.

• Use roasted whole chicken from the deli department of your local supermarket or vacuum-packed precooked chicken breasts when a recipe calls for cooked chicken.

• Freeze leftover broth in clean ice cube trays. Once the broth is frozen, remove the cubes and store them in a resealable freezer bag to prevent evaporation. Remove cubes as needed; they can be quickly defrosted in a microwave oven.

• Use packaged preshredded coleslaw mix or cabbage for egg roll fillings or any other recipes that call for shredded cabbage.

• Use chicken tenders for recipes that call for stir-frying strips of chicken. Turkey tenders, cutlets and tenderloin can be substituted for chicken cubes or strips.

Glossary of Chinese Ingredients

All of the recipes in this book were developed with Chinese ingredients that are generally available in large supermarkets. If you are unable to locate them in your store, you may also look for them in gourmet food stores and Oriental markets.

Bamboo shoots: tender, ivory-colored shoots of tropical bamboo plants, used separately as a vegetable and to add crispness and a slight sweetness to dishes. They are available fresh or in cans and should be rinsed with water before using. Store opened, canned bamboo shoots submerged in water in a covered container in the refrigerator. Every 2 to 3 days, drain and discard the water and replace it with fresh cold water. Bamboo shoots may be kept up to 2 weeks.

Bean sprouts: small white shoots of the pea-like mung bean plant, used separately as a vegetable and included in a wide variety of dishes. They are available fresh or in cans. Canned bean sprouts should be rinsed before use to eliminate any metallic taste. Store opened, canned bean sprouts submerged in water in a covered container in the refrigerator for up to 5 days. Store fresh bean sprouts in a plastic bag in the refrigerator for about 1 week.

Bean threads (also called cellophane noodles or Chinese rice vermicelli): dry, hard, white, fine noodles made from powdered mung beans. They have little flavor of their own, but readily absorb the flavors of other foods.

Bok choy: a member of the cabbage family, has white stalks and green, crinkled leaves. The woody stems take longer to cook than the delicate leaf tips. Store in a plastic bag in the refrigerator for up to 4 days.

Chili oil, hot: vegetable or sesame oil that has had hot red chilies steeped in it. This red-colored oil adds heat and flavor to Chinese dishes.

Egg noodles, Chinese: a thin pasta usually made of flour, egg, water and salt. The noodles can be purchased fresh, frozen or dried.

Egg roll wrappers: commercially prepared dough made of flour and water, rolled very thin and cut into 7- or 8-inch squares. They are available fresh or frozen.

Five-spice powder, Chinese: cocoa-colored powder that is a ready-mixed blend of five ground spices, usually anise seed, fennel seed, cloves, cinnamon and ginger or pepper. It has a slightly sweet, pungent flavor and should be used sparingly.

Ginger (also called ginger root): a knobby, gnarled root with a brown skin and whitish or light green interior. It has a fresh, pungent flavor and is used as a basic seasoning in many Chinese recipes. Ginger is available fresh and needs to be peeled before using. Store it wrapped in plastic in the refrigerator for about 2 weeks or in a resealable freezer bag in the freezer for up to 4 weeks. (You may cut off what you need and return the remainder to the freezer.) Or, store peeled ginger covered with dry sherry in an airtight container in the refrigerator for up to 6 months. The sherry absorbs some of the ginger flavor and may be used for cooking.

Hoisin sauce: a thick, dark brown sauce made of soybeans, flour, sugar, spices, garlic, chilies and salt. It has a sweet, spicy flavor and is called for in numerous Chinese recipes. It is available as a prepared sauce.

Mushrooms, dried: dehydrated black or brown mushrooms from the Orient, with caps from 1 to 3 inches in diameter. They have a strong distinctive flavor and are included in many different kinds of recipes. Chinese dried mushrooms must be soaked in warm water before using and are usually called for thinly sliced. Store in an airtight container in a cool, dark place.

Napa cabbage: a member of the cabbage family, has elongated tightly furled leaves, wide white ribs and soft pale green tips. Store in a closed plastic bag in the refrigerator for up to 5 days.

Oyster sauce: a thick, brown, concentrated sauce made of ground oysters, soy sauce and brine. It imparts very little fish flavor and is used as a seasoning to intensify other flavors. It is available as a prepared sauce.

Peanut oil: a golden-colored oil pressed from peanuts that has a light and slightly nutty flavor. This oil has a high smoke point that makes it ideal for using in stir-fried recipes. Store it tightly covered in a cool, dark place for up to 6 months after opening.

Plum sauce: a thick, piquant, chutney-like sauce frequently served with duck or pork dishes. It is available as a prepared sauce or can be homemade.

Sesame oil: an amber-colored oil pressed from toasted sesame seeds. It has a strong, nut-like flavor and is best used sparingly. Sesame oil is generally used as a flavoring, not as a cooking oil because of its low smoke point. Store it tightly covered in a cool, dark place for up to 2 months after opening.

Snow peas (also called pea pods or Chinese peas): flat, green pods that are picked before the peas have matured. They add crispness, color and flavor to foods, require very little cooking and are frequently used in stir-fried dishes. Snow peas are available fresh or frozen. Store fresh snow peas in a plastic bag in the refrigerator for 3 to 4 days.

Soy sauce: a pungent, brown, salty liquid made of fermented soybeans, wheat, yeast, salt and sometimes sugar. It is an essential ingredient in Chinese cooking. There are several types of soy sauce (light, dark, heavy), as well as Japanese-style soy sauce. The Japanese-style sauce is somewhere between the light and dark varieties. All types of soy sauce are available in bottles.

Stir-fry sauce: a prepared sauce that can be added as an instant seasoning to stir-fried dishes.

Sweet and sour sauce: a combination of sugar, vinegar and other flavorings. It is available as a prepared sauce or can be homemade.

Szechuan peppercorns: a reddish-brown pepper with a strong, pungent aroma and flavor. Its potent flavor has a time-delayed action and may not be noticed immediately. It is usually sold whole or crushed in small packages and should be used sparingly. Store it in an airtight container in a cool, dark place for up to 1 year.

Tofu (also called bean curd): puréed soybeans pressed to form a white, custard-like cake, used as a vegetable and as an excellent source of protein. Tofu can be used in all kinds of recipes because it readily absorbs the flavor of other foods. Tofu is available fresh. Store opened tofu submerged in water in a covered container in the refrigerator for up to 3 days. Drain and discard the water and replace it with fresh cold water daily. Tofu may also be stored tightly wrapped in plastic in the refrigerator for a few days.

Water chestnuts: walnut-sized bulbs from an aquatic plant. The bulb has a tough, brown skin and crisp, white interior. Water chestnuts are served separately as a vegetable and are used to add crisp texture and a delicate, sweet flavor to dishes. They are available fresh or in cans. Store opened, canned water chestnuts submerged in water in a covered container in the refrigerator for up to 1 week. Store fresh, unpeeled water chestnuts in a plastic bag in the refrigerator for up to 1 week.

Wonton wrappers: commercially prepared dough made of flour and water, rolled very thin and cut into 3- to 4-inch squares. They are available fresh or frozen.

APPETIZERS & SOUPS

WONTON SOUP

The ingredients for the wontons may be doubled. Use one batch now and freeze the second batch for a quick soup at a later date.

¼ pound ground pork, chicken or turkey
¼ cup finely chopped water chestnuts
2 tablespoons soy sauce, divided
1 teaspoon minced fresh ginger
1 egg white, slightly beaten
12 wonton wrappers

1 can (46 ounces) chicken broth
1½ cups sliced fresh spinach leaves
1 cup thinly sliced cooked pork (optional)
½ cup diagonally sliced green onions
1 tablespoon Oriental sesame oil
Shredded carrot for garnish

1. Combine ground pork, water chestnuts, 1 tablespoon soy sauce, ginger and egg white in small bowl; mix well.

2. Place 1 wonton wrapper with a point toward edge of counter. Mound 1 teaspoon of filling toward bottom point. Fold bottom point over filling, then roll wrapper over once. Moisten inside points with water. Bring side points together below the filling, overlapping slightly; press together firmly to seal. Repeat with remaining wrappers and filling.* Keep finished wontons covered with plastic wrap, while filling remaining wrappers.

3. Combine broth and remaining 1 tablespoon soy sauce in large saucepan. Bring to a boil over high heat. Reduce heat to medium; add wontons. Simmer, uncovered, 4 minutes.

4. Stir in spinach, cooked pork and onions; remove from heat. Stir in sesame oil. Ladle into soup bowls. Garnish with shredded carrot.

Makes 4 to 6 appetizer servings (about 7 cups)

Note: For information on storing unused water chestnuts, see page 7.

*Wontons may be made ahead to this point; cover and refrigerate up to 8 hours or freeze up to 3 months. Proceed as directed in step 3, if using refrigerated wontons. Increase simmer time to 6 minutes, if using frozen wontons.

Clockwise from top right: Wonton Soup, Easy Wonton Chips (page 10) and Beef Soup with Noodles (page 10)

EASY WONTON CHIPS

*These chips are so easy to make and are a great
accompaniment to soups or dips.*

1 tablespoon soy sauce
**2 teaspoons peanut or vegetable
oil**

½ teaspoon sugar
¼ teaspoon garlic salt
12 wonton wrappers

1. Preheat oven to 375°F.

2. Combine soy sauce, oil, sugar and garlic salt in small bowl; mix well.

3. Cut each wonton wrapper diagonally in half. Place wonton wrappers on 15×10-inch jelly-roll pan coated with nonstick cooking spray. Brush soy sauce mixture lightly but evenly over both sides of each wonton wrapper.

4. Bake 4 to 6 minutes or until crisp and lightly browned, turning after 3 minutes. Transfer to cooling rack; cool completely. *Makes 2 dozen chips*

BEEF SOUP WITH NOODLES

2 tablespoons soy sauce
1 teaspoon minced fresh ginger
**¼ teaspoon crushed red pepper
flakes**
**1 boneless beef top sirloin steak,
cut 1 inch thick (about
¾ pound)**
**1 tablespoon peanut or vegetable
oil**
2 cups sliced fresh mushrooms
**2 cans (about 14 ounces each) beef
broth**

**3 ounces (1 cup) fresh snow peas,
cut diagonally into 1-inch
pieces**
**1½ cups hot cooked fine egg noodles
(2 ounces uncooked)**
**1 green onion, cut diagonally into
thin slices**
**1 teaspoon Oriental sesame oil
(optional)**
**Red bell pepper strips for
garnish**
**Easy Wonton Chips (see above)
(optional)**

1. Combine soy sauce, ginger and crushed red pepper in small bowl. Spread mixture evenly over both sides of steak. Marinate at room temperature 15 minutes.

2. Heat deep skillet over medium-high heat. Add peanut oil; heat until hot. Drain steak; reserve soy sauce mixture (there will only be a small amount of mixture). Add steak to skillet; cook 4 to 5 minutes per side.* Let stand on cutting board 10 minutes.

3. Add mushrooms to skillet; stir-fry 2 minutes. Add broth, snow peas and reserved soy sauce mixture; bring to a boil, scraping up browned meat bits. Reduce heat to medium-low. Stir in noodles.

4. Cut steak across the grain into ⅛-inch slices; cut each slice into 1-inch pieces. Stir into soup; heat through. Stir in onion and sesame oil. Ladle into soup bowls. Garnish with red pepper strips. Serve with Easy Wonton Chips.
Makes 4 main-dish or 6 appetizer servings (about 6 cups)

*Cooking time is for medium-rare doneness. Adjust time for desired doneness.

CHINATOWN STUFFED MUSHROOMS

24 large fresh mushrooms (about 1 pound)
½ pound ground pork or turkey
1 clove garlic, minced
¼ cup fine dry bread crumbs
¼ cup thinly sliced green onions

3 tablespoons soy sauce, divided
1 teaspoon minced fresh ginger
1 egg white, slightly beaten
⅛ teaspoon crushed red pepper flakes (optional)

1. Remove stems from mushrooms; finely chop enough stems to equal 1 cup. Reserve remaining stems for use in salads, soups or stews, if desired. Cook pork with chopped stems and garlic in medium skillet over medium-high heat until pork is no longer pink, stirring to separate pork. Spoon off fat.

2. Stir in bread crumbs, onions, 2 tablespoons soy sauce, ginger, egg white and crushed red pepper; mix well.

3. Brush mushrooms lightly on all sides with remaining 1 tablespoon soy sauce; spoon about 2 teaspoons stuffing into each mushroom cap.* Place stuffed mushrooms on rack of foil-lined broiler pan. Broil 4 to 5 inches from heat 5 to 6 minutes until hot.

Makes 2 dozen appetizers

*Mushrooms may be made ahead to this point; cover and refrigerate up to 24 hours. Increase broiling time by 1 to 2 minutes for the chilled mushrooms.

ORIENTAL CHICKEN WINGS

These wings are an Oriental version of the popular Buffalo Wings.

12 chicken wings *or* 24 chicken drumettes
¼ cup *plus* 2 teaspoons soy sauce, divided
2 tablespoons dry sherry

2 cloves garlic, minced
2 teaspoons brown sugar
½ cup lite or fat-free mayonnaise
1 teaspoon rice vinegar
½ teaspoon Oriental sesame oil

1. Cut off chicken wing tips at joint; discard tips or save for making chicken broth. Cut each remaining wing portion at other joint to make 2 pieces. Place in large plastic bag.

2. Combine ¼ cup soy sauce, sherry, garlic and brown sugar in cup; pour over chicken wings. Close bag securely; turn to coat. Marinate in refrigerator at least 4 hours or up to 24 hours.

3. Combine mayonnaise, vinegar, sesame oil and remaining 2 teaspoons soy sauce in small bowl. Cover and refrigerate until ready to serve.

4. Drain chicken wings; reserve marinade. Place wings on rack of broiler pan. Brush with half of reserved marinade. Broil 6 inches from heat 10 minutes. Turn wings over; brush with remaining marinade. Broil 10 minutes or until chicken is browned and cooked through. Serve mayonnaise mixture as a dipping sauce for wings.

Makes 2 dozen appetizers

SPICY CHICKEN BUNDLES

1 pound ground chicken or turkey
2 teaspoons minced fresh ginger
2 cloves garlic, minced
¼ teaspoon crushed red pepper flakes
3 tablespoons soy sauce
1 tablespoon cornstarch
1 tablespoon peanut or vegetable oil

⅓ cup finely chopped water chestnuts
⅓ cup thinly sliced green onions
¼ cup chopped peanuts
12 large lettuce leaves, such as romaine
Chinese hot mustard (optional)

1. Combine chicken, ginger, garlic and crushed red pepper in medium bowl.

2. Blend soy sauce into cornstarch in cup until smooth.

3. Heat wok or large skillet over medium-high heat. Add oil; heat until hot. Add chicken mixture; stir-fry 2 to 3 minutes until chicken is no longer pink.

4. Stir soy sauce mixture and add to wok. Stir-fry 30 seconds or until sauce boils and thickens. Add water chestnuts, onions and peanuts; heat through.*

5. Divide filling evenly among lettuce leaves; roll up. Secure with wooden toothpicks. Serve warm or at room temperature. Do not let filling stand at room temperature more than 2 hours. Serve with hot mustard.   *Makes 12 appetizers*

Note: For information on storing unused water chestnuts, see page 7.

*Filling may be made ahead to this point; cover and refrigerate up to 4 hours. Just before rolling in lettuce, reheat chicken filling until warm. Proceed as directed in step 5.

SPRING ROLLS

Flour tortillas make these no-cook Spring Rolls so easy to prepare!

1 cup preshredded cabbage or coleslaw mix
½ cup finely chopped cooked ham
¼ cup finely chopped water chestnuts

¼ cup thinly sliced green onions
3 tablespoons plum sauce, divided
1 teaspoon Oriental sesame oil
3 flour tortillas (6 to 7 inches)

1. Combine cabbage, ham, water chestnuts, onions, 2 tablespoons plum sauce and sesame oil in medium bowl; mix well.

2. Spread remaining 1 tablespoon plum sauce evenly over tortillas. Spread about ½ cup cabbage mixture on each tortilla to within ¼ inch of edge; roll up.

3. Wrap each tortilla tightly in plastic wrap. Refrigerate at least 1 hour or up to 24 hours before serving.

4. Cut each tortilla diagonally into 4 pieces.   *Makes 12 appetizers*

Note: For information on storing unused water chestnuts, see page 7.

Top to bottom: Spicy Chicken Bundles and Spring Rolls

HOT AND SOUR SOUP

Leftovers from Roasted Pork, Chinese Barbecued Pork or Crispy Roasted Chicken are ideal to use for this spicy soup.

1 package (1 ounce) dried black Chinese mushrooms*
4 ounces firm tofu, drained
4 cups chicken broth
3 tablespoons white vinegar
2 tablespoons soy sauce
½ to 1 teaspoon hot chili oil
¼ teaspoon ground white pepper
1 cup shredded cooked pork, chicken or turkey

½ cup drained canned bamboo shoots, cut into thin strips
3 tablespoons water
2 tablespoons cornstarch
1 egg white, slightly beaten
¼ cup thinly sliced green onions or chopped cilantro
1 teaspoon Oriental sesame oil

1. Place mushrooms in small bowl; cover with warm water. Soak 20 minutes to soften. Drain; squeeze out excess water. Discard stems; slice caps. Press tofu lightly between paper towels; cut into ½-inch squares or triangles.

2. Combine broth, vinegar, soy sauce, chili oil and pepper in medium saucepan. Bring to a boil over high heat. Reduce heat to medium. Simmer 2 minutes.

3. Stir in mushrooms, tofu, pork and bamboo shoots; heat through.

4. Blend water into cornstarch in cup until smooth. Stir into soup. Cook and stir 4 minutes or until soup boils and thickens.

5. Remove from heat. Stirring constantly in one direction, slowly pour egg white in a thin stream into soup. Stir in onions and sesame oil. Ladle into soup bowls.

Makes 4 to 6 appetizer servings (about 6 cups)

Note: For information on storing unused bamboo shoots and tofu, see pages 6 and 7.

*Or, substitute 2 cups sliced fresh mushrooms. Omit soaking mushrooms in step 1.

ORIENTAL SALSA

Here's an Oriental twist to a Tex-Mex favorite.

1 cup diced, unpeeled cucumber
½ cup chopped red bell pepper
½ cup thinly sliced green onions
⅓ cup coarsely chopped cilantro
1 clove garlic, minced
1 tablespoon rice vinegar

2 teaspoons soy sauce
½ teaspoon Oriental sesame oil
¼ teaspoon crushed red pepper flakes
Easy Wonton Chips (page 10) or Chinese crackers

1. Combine all ingredients except Easy Wonton Chips in medium bowl until well blended.

2. Cover and refrigerate until serving time. Serve with Easy Wonton Chips for dipping. Or, use salsa as an accompaniment to broiled fish, chicken or pork.

Makes 1½ cups salsa

CHILLED SHRIMP IN CHINESE MUSTARD SAUCE

1 cup water
½ cup dry white wine
2 tablespoons soy sauce
½ teaspoon Szechuan or black peppercorns

1 pound large raw shrimp, peeled, deveined
¼ cup sweet and sour sauce
2 teaspoons Chinese hot mustard

1. Combine water, wine, soy sauce and peppercorns in medium saucepan. Bring to a boil over high heat. Add shrimp; reduce heat to medium. Cover and simmer 2 to 3 minutes until shrimp are opaque. Drain well. Cover and refrigerate until chilled.

2. Combine sweet and sour sauce and hot mustard in small bowl; mix well. Serve as a dipping sauce for shrimp.   *Makes 6 appetizer servings*

EGG ROLLS

¼ cup soy sauce
2 tablespoons dry sherry
4 teaspoons cornstarch
   Peanut or vegetable oil
6 cups chopped or shredded cabbage *or* preshredded coleslaw mix or cabbage (about 12 ounces)
1 cup chopped fresh mushrooms
⅔ cup thinly sliced green onions

½ pound ground beef, pork or turkey
3 cloves garlic, minced
¼ teaspoon crushed red pepper flakes
12 egg roll wrappers *or* 24 wonton wrappers
   Sweet and sour sauce for dipping
   Chinese hot mustard (optional)

1. Blend soy sauce and sherry into cornstarch in cup until smooth.

2. Heat wok or large skillet over medium-high heat. Add 1 tablespoon oil; heat until hot. Add cabbage, mushrooms and onions; stir-fry 2 minutes (cabbage will still be crisp). Remove; set aside.

3. Add beef, garlic and crushed red pepper to wok; cook until beef is no longer pink, stirring to separate beef. Spoon off fat.

4. Stir soy sauce mixture and add to wok. Stir-fry 2 minutes or until sauce boils and thickens. Return cabbage mixture; heat through, mixing well.*

5. Place each egg roll wrapper with one point toward edge of counter. Spoon filling across and just below center of wrapper; use heaping ⅓ cup filling for each egg roll wrapper or 2 teaspoons filling for each wonton wrapper.

6. To form egg roll, fold bottom point of wrapper up over filling. Fold side points over filling, forming an envelope shape. Moisten inside edges of top point with water and roll egg roll toward that point, pressing firmly to seal. Repeat with remaining wrappers and filling.

7. Pour ½ inch oil into large skillet. Heat oil to 375°F. Fry egg rolls, 2 or 3 at a time, or mini-egg rolls, 6 to 8 at time, 2 minutes per side or until crisp and golden brown. Drain on paper towels. Serve with sweet and sour sauce and hot mustard.
                            Makes about 12 egg rolls or 24 mini-egg rolls

*Egg roll filling may be made ahead to this point; cover and refrigerate up to 24 hours. When ready to use, heat mixture until hot. Proceed as directed in step 5.

MARINATED VEGETABLES

⅓ cup peanut or vegetable oil
3 tablespoons rice vinegar
2 tablespoons soy sauce
1 clove garlic, minced
1 teaspoon minced fresh ginger
½ teaspoon sugar
2 cups broccoli florets

2 cups cauliflower florets
2 cups diagonally sliced carrots
   (½-inch pieces)
½ pound fresh mushrooms
1 large red bell pepper, cut into
   1-inch pieces
Lettuce leaves (optional)

1. Combine oil, vinegar, soy sauce, garlic, ginger and sugar in large bowl.

2. To blanch broccoli, cauliflower and carrots, cook 1 minute in salted boiling water to cover. Plunge into cold water, then drain immediately. Toss with oil mixture while still warm. Cool to room temperature.

3. Add mushrooms and red pepper to bowl; toss to coat. Cover and marinate in refrigerator at least 4 hours or up to 24 hours. Drain vegetables; reserve marinade. Arrange vegetables on lettuce-lined platter. Serve chilled or at room temperature with wooden toothpicks. If desired, serve reserved marinade in small cup for dipping.
Makes 12 to 16 appetizer servings

MINI-MARINATED BEEF SKEWERS

1 boneless beef sirloin steak, cut 1
   inch thick (about 1 pound)
2 tablespoons soy sauce
2 tablespoons dry sherry

1 tablespoon Oriental sesame oil
2 cloves garlic, minced
18 cherry tomatoes
   Lettuce leaves (optional)

1. Cut beef across the grain into ⅛-inch slices. Place in large plastic bag. Combine soy sauce, sherry, sesame oil and garlic in cup; pour over steak. Close bag securely; turn to coat. Marinate in refrigerator at least 30 minutes or up to 2 hours.

2. Soak 18 (6-inch) wooden skewers in water to cover 20 minutes.

3. Drain steak; discard marinade. Weave beef accordion-fashion onto skewers. Place on rack of broiler pan.

4. Broil 4 to 5 inches from heat 2 minutes. Turn skewers over; broil 2 minutes or until beef is barely pink in center.

5. Garnish each skewer with one cherry tomato; place on lettuce-lined platter. Serve warm or at room temperature.
Makes 18 appetizers

SHRIMP TOAST

Shrimp Toast, a perennial favorite of Chinese cuisine, can be easily prepared at home following this delicious recipe.

½ pound raw shrimp, peeled, deveined
2 tablespoons chopped green onion
2 tablespoons finely chopped water chestnuts
2 tablespoons soy sauce

1 teaspoon Oriental sesame oil
1 egg white, slightly beaten
6 slices white sandwich bread, crusts removed
Red and yellow bell peppers for garnish

1. Finely chop shrimp. If using food processor, process with on/off pulses, about 10 times or until shrimp are finely chopped.

2. Combine shrimp, onion, water chestnuts, soy sauce and sesame oil in medium bowl; mix well. Stir in egg white; mix well.*

3. Toast bread lightly on both sides. Cut toast diagonally into quarters. Spread shrimp mixture evenly over toast to edges.

4. Place toast on foil-lined baking sheet or broiler pan. Broil 6 inches from heat 4 minutes or until lightly browned. Garnish with peppers.

Makes 2 dozen appetizers

Note: For information on storing unused water chestnuts, see page 7.

*The filling may be made ahead to this point; cover and refrigerate filling up to 24 hours. Proceed as directed in step 3.

CHICKEN AND CORN SOUP

1 can (17 ounces) cream-style corn
1 can (about 14 ounces) chicken broth
1½ cups shredded cooked chicken or turkey
1 tablespoon soy sauce

1 tablespoon dry sherry
1 teaspoon minced fresh ginger
⅛ teaspoon ground white pepper
1 teaspoon Oriental sesame oil (optional)
¼ cup thinly sliced green onions

1. Combine corn, broth, chicken, soy sauce, sherry, ginger and pepper in large saucepan. Bring to a boil over high heat. Reduce heat to medium-low.

2. Simmer, uncovered, 5 minutes; remove from heat. Stir in sesame oil. Sprinkle with onions. Ladle into soup bowls.

Makes 4 appetizer servings (about 5 cups)

Shrimp Toast

EGG DROP SOUP

This traditional Chinese soup is super easy to make!

2 cans (about 14 ounces each)
    chicken broth
1 tablespoon soy sauce
2 teaspoons cornstarch

1 egg
1 egg white
¼ cup thinly sliced green onions

1. Heat broth in large saucepan over high heat until hot; reduce heat so that broth simmers gently.

2. Blend soy sauce into cornstarch in cup until smooth; stir into broth. Cook and stir 2 minutes or until soup boils and thickens slightly.

3. Beat egg with egg white in small bowl. Stirring constantly in one direction, slowly pour egg mixture in a thin stream into soup.

4. Ladle into soup bowls. Sprinkle with onions.

Makes 4 appetizer servings (about 3½ cups)

SPICY BEEF TURNOVERS

½ pound lean ground beef or
    turkey
2 cloves garlic, minced
2 tablespoons soy sauce
1 tablespoon water
½ teaspoon cornstarch
1 teaspoon curry powder
¼ teaspoon Chinese five-spice
    powder

¼ teaspoon crushed red pepper
    flakes
2 tablespoons minced green onion
1 package (7.5 ounces)
    refrigerated biscuits
1 egg
1 tablespoon water

1. Preheat oven to 400°F. Cook beef with garlic in medium skillet over medium-high heat until beef is no longer pink, stirring to separate beef. Spoon off fat.

2. Blend soy sauce and water into cornstarch in cup until smooth. Add soy sauce mixture along with curry powder, five-spice powder and crushed red pepper to skillet. Cook and stir 30 seconds or until liquid is absorbed, stirring constantly. Remove from heat; stir in onion.

3. Roll each biscuit between 2 sheets of waxed paper into 4-inch rounds. Spoon heaping 1 tablespoon beef mixture onto one side of each biscuit; fold over, forming a semi-circle. Pinch edges together to seal.*

4. Arrange turnovers on baking sheet coated with nonstick cooking spray. Beat egg with water in cup; brush lightly over turnovers. Bake 9 to 10 minutes until golden brown. Serve warm or at room temperature. *Makes 10 appetizers*

*At this point, turnovers may be wrapped and frozen up to 3 months. Thaw completely before proceeding as directed in step 4.

CRAB CAKES CANTON

½ pound thawed frozen cooked
    crabmeat *or* imitation
    crabmeat, drained and flaked
    or finely chopped (about
    2 cups)
1½ cups fresh bread crumbs
¼ cup thinly sliced green onions

1 clove garlic, minced
1 teaspoon minced fresh ginger
2 egg whites, slightly beaten
3 tablespoons oyster sauce
4 teaspoons peanut or vegetable
    oil, divided
Sweet and sour sauce

1. Combine crabmeat, bread crumbs, onions, garlic and ginger in medium bowl; mix well. Add egg whites and oyster sauce; mix well.

2. Shape into 12 patties, about ½ inch thick and 2 inches in diameter.* Heat large nonstick skillet over medium heat. Add 2 teaspoons oil; heat until hot.

3. Cook 6 crab cakes in hot oil 2 minutes per side or until golden brown. Remove to warm serving plate; keep warm. Repeat with remaining oil and crab cakes. Serve with sweet and sour sauce.
Makes 12 appetizers

Notes: To reheat cooked crab cakes, place in single layer on baking sheet. Bake in preheated 350°F oven 9 to 10 minutes until heated through.

Crab mixture may also be shaped into 6 large cakes, ½ inch thick and 3½ inches in diameter. Cook 3 crab cakes at one time as directed in recipe.

*Crab mixture may be made ahead to this point; cover and refrigerate up to 24 hours before cooking. Proceed as directed in step 2.

SHANTUNG TWIN MUSHROOM SOUP

1 package (1 ounce) dried black
    Chinese mushrooms*
1 tablespoon peanut or vegetable
    oil
1 large onion, coarsely chopped
2 cloves garlic, minced
2 cups sliced fresh mushrooms

2 cans (about 14 ounces each)
    chicken broth
2 ounces cooked ham, cut into thin
    slivers (½ cup)
½ cup thinly sliced green onions
1 tablespoon soy sauce
1 tablespoon dry sherry
1 tablespoon cornstarch

1. Place dried mushrooms in small bowl; cover with warm water. Soak 20 minutes to soften. Drain; squeeze out excess water. Discard stems; slice caps.

2. Heat large saucepan over medium heat. Add oil; heat until hot. Add chopped onion and garlic; cook 1 minute. Add both mushrooms; cook 4 minutes, stirring occasionally.

3. Add broth; bring to a boil over high heat. Reduce heat to medium-low. Cover and simmer 15 minutes.

4. Stir in ham and green onions; heat through. Blend soy sauce and sherry into cornstarch in cup until smooth. Stir into soup. Cook 2 minutes or until soup thickens, stirring occasionally. Ladle into soup bowls.
Makes 6 appetizer servings (about 5½ cups)

*Or, substitute 4 ounces fresh shiitake mushrooms; discard stems and slice caps. Omit step 1.

MEATS

PEPPER BEEF

This makes a colorful entrée.

1 tablespoon soy sauce
2 cloves garlic, minced
¼ teaspoon crushed red pepper
flakes
1 boneless beef sirloin, tenderloin
or rib eye steak, cut 1 inch
thick (about 1 pound)
2 tablespoons peanut or vegetable
oil, divided
1 small red bell pepper, cut into
thin strips

1 small yellow or green bell
pepper, cut into thin strips
1 small onion, cut into thin strips
¼ cup stir-fry sauce
2 tablespoons rice wine or dry
white wine
¼ cup coarsely chopped cilantro
Hot cooked white rice or Chinese
egg noodles (optional)

1. Combine soy sauce, garlic and crushed red pepper in medium bowl. Cut beef across the grain into ⅛-inch slices; cut each slice into 1½-inch pieces. Toss beef with soy sauce mixture.

2. Heat wok or large skillet over medium-high heat. Add 1 tablespoon oil; heat until hot. Add half of beef mixture; stir-fry until beef is barely pink in center. Remove and reserve. Repeat with remaining beef mixture; remove and reserve.

3. Heat remaining 1 tablespoon oil in wok; add bell peppers and onion. Reduce heat to medium. Stir-fry 6 to 7 minutes until vegetables are crisp-tender. Add stir-fry sauce and wine; stir-fry 2 minutes or until heated through.

4. Return beef along with any accumulated juices to wok; heat through. Sprinkle with cilantro. Serve over rice.
Makes 4 servings

BARBECUED RIBS

3 to 4 pounds lean pork baby back
    ribs or spareribs
⅓ cup hoisin sauce
4 tablespoons soy sauce, divided

3 tablespoons dry sherry
3 cloves garlic, minced
2 tablespoons honey
1 tablespoon Oriental sesame oil

1. Place ribs in large plastic bag. Combine hoisin sauce, 3 tablespoons soy sauce, sherry and garlic in cup; pour over ribs. Close bag securely; turn to coat. Marinate in refrigerator at least 4 hours or up to 24 hours.

2. Preheat oven to 375°F. Drain ribs; reserve marinade. Place ribs on rack in shallow, foil-lined roasting pan. Cook 30 minutes. Turn; brush ribs with half of reserved marinade. Cook 15 minutes. Turn ribs over; brush with remaining marinade. Cook 15 minutes.

3. Combine remaining 1 tablespoon soy sauce, honey and sesame oil in small bowl; brush over ribs. Cook 5 to 10 minutes until ribs are browned and crisp.* Cut into serving-size pieces. *Makes 4 main-dish or 8 appetizer servings*

*Ribs may be made ahead to this point; cover and refrigerate ribs up to 3 days. To reheat ribs, wrap in foil; cook in preheated 350°F oven 40 minutes or until heated through. Cut into serving-size pieces.

BEEF WITH BEAN THREADS AND CABBAGE

1 package (3¾ ounces) bean
    threads
1 boneless beef sirloin steak, cut
    1 inch thick (about 1 pound)
2 cloves garlic, minced
1 teaspoon minced fresh ginger

1 tablespoon peanut or vegetable
    oil
½ cup beef or chicken broth
2 tablespoons oyster sauce
2 cups coarsely chopped napa
    cabbage

1. Place bean threads in medium bowl; cover with warm water. Soak 15 minutes to soften; drain well. Cut into 2-inch lengths.

2. Cut beef across grain into ⅛-inch slices; cut each slice into 2-inch pieces. Toss beef with garlic and ginger in medium bowl.

3. Heat wok or large skillet over medium-high heat. Add oil; heat until hot. Add beef mixture; stir-fry 2 to 3 minutes until beef is barely pink in center. Add broth, oyster sauce and cabbage; stir-fry 1 minute. Add bean threads; stir-fry 1 to 2 minutes until liquid is absorbed. *Makes 4 servings*

Barbecued Ribs

PORK WITH THREE ONIONS

⅓ cup teriyaki sauce
2 cloves garlic, minced
1 pound pork tenderloin
2 tablespoons peanut or vegetable
   oil, divided
1 small red onion, cut into thin
   wedges

1 small yellow onion, cut into thin
   wedges
1 teaspoon sugar
1 teaspoon cornstarch
2 green onions, cut into 1-inch
   pieces
Fried bean threads* (optional)

1. Combine teriyaki sauce and garlic in shallow bowl. Cut pork across the grain into ¼-inch slices; cut each slice in half. Toss pork with teriyaki mixture. Marinate at room temperature 10 minutes.

2. Heat large skillet over medium-high heat. Add 1 tablespoon oil; heat until hot. Drain pork; reserve marinade. Stir-fry pork 3 minutes or until no longer pink. Remove and reserve.

3. Heat remaining 1 tablespoon oil in skillet; add red and yellow onions. Reduce heat to medium. Cook 4 to 5 minutes until softened, stirring occasionally. Sprinkle with sugar; cook 1 minute more.

4. Blend reserved marinade into cornstarch in cup until smooth. Stir into skillet. Stir-fry 1 minute or until sauce boils and thickens.

5. Return pork along with any accumulated juices to skillet; heat through. Stir in green onions. Serve over bean threads.   *Makes 4 servings*

*To fry bean threads, follow package directions.

FRAGRANT BEEF WITH GARLIC SAUCE

1 boneless beef top sirloin steak,
   cut 1 inch thick (about
   1¼ pounds)

⅓ cup teriyaki sauce
10 large cloves garlic, peeled
½ cup beef broth

1. Place beef in large plastic bag. Pour teriyaki sauce over beef. Close bag securely; turn to coat. Marinate in refrigerator at least 30 minutes or up to 4 hours.

2. Combine garlic and broth in small saucepan. Bring to a boil over high heat. Reduce heat to medium. Simmer, uncovered, 5 minutes. Cover and simmer 8 to 9 minutes until garlic is softened. Transfer to blender or food processor; process until smooth.

3. Meanwhile, drain beef; reserve marinade. Place beef on rack of broiler pan. Brush with half of reserved marinade. Broil 5 to 6 inches from heat 5 minutes. Turn beef over; brush with remaining marinade. Broil 5 minutes.*

4. Slice beef thinly; serve with garlic sauce.   *Makes 4 servings*

*Broiling time is for medium-rare doneness. Adjust time for desired doneness.

Pork with Three Onions

ORANGE BEEF

1 boneless beef sirloin or
   tenderloin steak, cut 1 inch
   thick (about 1 pound)
2 cloves garlic, minced
1 teaspoon grated *fresh* orange
   peel
2 tablespoons soy sauce
2 tablespoons orange juice

1 tablespoon dry sherry
1 tablespoon cornstarch
1 tablespoon peanut or vegetable
   oil
2 cups hot cooked white rice
   (optional)
Orange slices for garnish

1. Cut beef across the grain into ⅛-inch slices; cut each slice into 2-inch pieces. Toss with garlic and orange peel in medium bowl.

2. Blend soy sauce, orange juice and sherry into cornstarch in cup until smooth.

3. Heat wok or large skillet over medium-high heat. Add oil; heat until hot. Add beef mixture; stir-fry 2 to 3 minutes or until beef is barely pink in center. Stir soy sauce mixture and add to wok. Stir-fry 30 seconds or until sauce boils and thickens. Serve over rice. Garnish with orange slices.

Makes 4 servings

MONGOLIAN HOT POT

With this fondue-like dish, each person cooks their own dinner in a simmering broth. When all the food is cooked, spinach is added to the broth. Then the broth is served over bean threads in soup bowls.

2 ounces bean threads
1 boneless beef sirloin or
   tenderloin steak, cut 1 inch
   thick (about ½ pound)
1 can (46 ounces) chicken broth
½ pound pork tenderloin, cut into
   ⅛-inch slices

½ pound medium raw shrimp,
   peeled, deveined
½ pound sea scallops, cut
   lengthwise into halves
½ pound small fresh mushrooms
   Dipping Sauce (recipe follows)
1 pound spinach leaves

1. Place bean threads in medium bowl; cover with warm water. Soak 15 minutes to soften; drain well. Cut bean threads into 1- to 2-inch lengths; set aside.

2. Cut beef across the grain into ⅛-inch slices; cut each slice into 1½-inch pieces.

3. Heat broth in electric skillet to a simmer (or, heat half of broth in fondue pot, keeping remaining broth hot for replacement).

4. Arrange beef, pork, shrimp, scallops and mushrooms on large platter.

5. Prepare Dipping Sauce.

6. To serve, select food from platter and cook it in simmering broth until desired doneness, using chop sticks or long-handled fork. Dip into dipping sauce before eating.

6. After all the food is cooked, stir spinach into broth and heat until wilted. (Cook spinach in two batches if using a fondue pot.) Place bean threads in individual soup bowls. Ladle broth mixture into bowls. Season with dipping sauce, if desired.

Makes 4 to 6 servings

Dipping Sauce: Combine ½ cup lite soy sauce, ¼ cup dry sherry and 1 tablespoon Oriental sesame oil in small bowl; divide into individual dipping bowls.

HONEY-GLAZED PORK

**1 large *or* 2 small pork tenderloins
  (about 1¼ pounds total
  weight)**
¼ cup soy sauce
2 cloves garlic, minced

3 tablespoons honey
2 tablespoons brown sugar
1 teaspoon minced fresh ginger
**1 tablespoon toasted sesame
  seeds***

1. Place pork in large plastic bag. Combine soy sauce and garlic in small cup; pour over pork. Close bag securely; turn to coat. Marinate in refrigerator up to 2 hours.

2. Preheat oven to 400°F. Drain pork; reserve 1 tablespoon marinade. Combine honey, brown sugar, ginger and reserved marinade in small bowl.

3. Place pork in shallow, foil-lined roasting pan. Brush with half of honey mixture. Roast 10 minutes. Turn pork over; brush with remaining honey mixture and sprinkle with sesame seeds. Roast 10 minutes for small or 15 minutes for large tenderloin or until internal temperature reaches 155°F when tested with a meat thermometer inserted in thickest part of pork.

4. Let pork stand, tented with foil, on cutting board 5 minutes. (Temperature will rise to 160°F.) Pour pan juices into serving pitcher. Cut pork across the grain into ½-inch slices. Serve with pan juices. *Makes 4 servings*

*To toast sesame seeds, spread seeds in small skillet. Shake skillet over medium heat 2 minutes or until seeds begin to pop and turn golden.

MING DYNASTY BEEF STEW

**2 pounds boneless beef chuck or
  veal shoulder, cut into 1½-inch
  pieces**
**1 teaspoon Chinese five-spice
  powder**
**½ teaspoon crushed red pepper
  flakes**
**2 tablespoons peanut or vegetable
  oil, divided**
1 large onion, coarsely chopped
2 cloves garlic, minced

1 cup beef broth
1 cup regular or light beer
2 tablespoons soy sauce
1 tablespoon cornstarch
  **Hot cooked Chinese egg noodles
    or Sesame Noodle Cake
    (page 78)**
  **Grated lemon peel, chopped
    cilantro *and/or* chopped
    peanuts for garnish**

1. Sprinkle beef with five-spice powder and crushed red pepper. Heat large saucepan or Dutch oven over medium-high heat. Add 1 tablespoon oil; heat until hot. Add half of beef; brown on all sides. Remove and reserve. Repeat with remaining oil and beef.

2. Add onion and garlic to saucepan; cook 3 minutes, stirring occasionally. Add broth and beer; bring to a boil. Reduce heat to medium-low. Return beef along with any accumulated juices to saucepan; cover and simmer 1 hour and 15 minutes or until beef is fork tender.*

3. Blend soy sauce into cornstarch in cup until smooth. Stir into saucepan. Cook, uncovered, 2 minutes or until mixture thickens, stirring occasionally. Serve over noodles. Garnish as desired. *Makes 6 to 8 servings*

*Stew may be oven-braised if saucepan or Dutch oven is ovenproof. Cover and bake in 350°F oven 1 hour and 15 minutes or until beef is fork tender. Proceed as directed in step 3.

SPICY BEEF WITH NOODLES

This dish is perfect for make-ahead entertaining and is easy to transport. It is great for a buffet, since the flavors are best when served at room temperature.

1 package (1 ounce) dried black Chinese mushrooms*

6 tablespoons peanut or vegetable oil, divided

2 teaspoons minced fresh ginger

2 large cloves garlic, minced

½ teaspoon crushed red pepper flakes

2 tablespoons soy sauce

2 tablespoons rice vinegar

1 teaspoon Oriental sesame oil

1 boneless beef top sirloin steak, cut 1 inch thick (about 1 pound)

1 red bell pepper, cut into short, thin strips

5 ounces (1½ cups) fresh snow peas, cut lengthwise into thin strips

8 ounces vermicelli or thin spaghetti, broken in half *or* somen noodles, cooked and drained

Coarsely chopped roasted cashews (optional)

1. Place mushrooms in small bowl; cover with warm water. Soak 20 minutes to soften. Drain; squeeze out excess water. Discard stems; slice caps.

2. Combine 2 tablespoons peanut oil, ginger, garlic and crushed red pepper in small bowl. Spread 2 teaspoons oil mixture evenly over both sides of steak. Marinate at room temperature 15 minutes or cover and refrigerate up to 24 hours. Stir soy sauce, vinegar, 3 tablespoons peanut oil and sesame oil into remaining oil mixture; set aside.

3. Heat large, deep nonstick skillet over medium to medium-high heat until hot. Add steak; cook 4 to 5 minutes per side.** Let stand on cutting board 10 minutes.

4. Heat remaining 1 tablespoon peanut oil in skillet over medium heat. Add mushrooms, red bell pepper and snow peas; stir-fry 3 to 4 minutes until vegetables are crisp-tender.

5. Toss hot cooked vermicelli with reserved oil mixture in large bowl. Cut steak across the grain into ⅛-inch slices; cut each slice into 1½-inch pieces. Add steak along with any accumulated juices to noodle mixture. Add vegetables; toss well. Serve warm, at room temperature or chilled. Just before serving, sprinkle with cashews.

Makes 4 to 6 servings

*Or, substitute 4 ounces fresh shiitake mushrooms; discard stems and slice caps. Omit step 1.

**Cooking time is for medium-rare doneness. Adjust time for desired doneness.

Spicy Beef with Noodles

BEEF AND BROCCOLI

1 boneless beef top sirloin or
    tenderloin steak, cut 1 inch
    thick (about 1 pound)
2 teaspoons minced fresh ginger
2 cloves garlic, minced
1 tablespoon peanut or vegetable
    oil

3 cups broccoli florets
¼ cup water
⅓ cup stir-fry sauce
    Hot cooked white rice (optional)

1. Cut beef across the grain into ⅛-inch slices; cut each slice into 1½-inch pieces. Toss beef with ginger and garlic in medium bowl.

2. Heat wok or large skillet over medium-high heat. Add oil; heat until hot. Add beef mixture; stir-fry 3 to 4 minutes until beef is barely pink in center. Remove and reserve.

3. Add broccoli and water to wok; cover and steam 3 to 5 minutes until broccoli is crisp-tender.

4. Return beef along with any accumulated juices to wok. Add stir-fry sauce. Cook until heated through. Serve over rice.   *Makes 4 servings*

GLAZED PORK AND PEPPER KABOBS

1 pound lean boneless pork loin,
    cut into 1½-inch pieces
1 large red bell pepper, cut into
    1-inch pieces
1 large yellow bell pepper, cut into
    1-inch pieces

1 large green bell pepper, cut into
    1-inch pieces
¼ cup soy sauce
3 cloves garlic, minced
¼ cup sweet and sour sauce
1 tablespoon Chinese hot mustard

1. Place pork and peppers in large plastic bag. Combine soy sauce and garlic in cup; pour over meat and peppers. Close bag securely; turn to coat. Marinate in refrigerator at least 30 minutes or up to 2 hours, turning once.

2. Drain meat and peppers; discard marinade. Alternately thread meat and peppers onto metal skewers.

3. Combine sweet and sour sauce and hot mustard in small bowl; reserve half of sauce for dipping. Grill or broil kabobs 5 to 6 inches from heat 14 to 16 minutes until pork is no longer pink, turning occasionally and brushing with remaining sauce mixture during last 5 minutes of cooking. Serve with reserved sauce.   *Makes 4 servings*

Beef and Broccoli

STIR-FRIED PORK AND VEGETABLES

*Baby corn cobs are tender, miniature ears of corn that can be completely eaten.
They are also great in soups and salads.*

1 pound lean boneless pork loin or
    tenderloin roast
2 cloves garlic, minced
2 teaspoons minced fresh ginger
2 tablespoons peanut or vegetable
    oil, divided
1 jar (7 ounces) baby corn cobs,
    drained and rinsed

6 ounces (2 cups) fresh snow peas
    or 1 package (6 ounces) frozen
    snow peas, thawed and cut
    into halves, if large
½ cup stir-fry sauce
    Hot cooked white rice or Chinese
    egg noodles (optional)

1. Cut pork across the grain into ¼-inch slices; cut each slice into 1¼×¼-inch strips.
Toss pork with garlic and ginger in small bowl.

2. Heat wok or large skillet over medium-high heat. Add 1 tablespoon oil; heat until
hot. Add pork mixture; stir-fry 3 minutes or until pork is no longer pink. Remove and
reserve.

3. Heat remaining 1 tablespoon oil in wok. Add corn cobs and snow peas; stir-fry
3 minutes for fresh or 2 minutes for frozen snow peas or until crisp-tender and corn
cobs are hot. Add stir-fry sauce; stir-fry 30 seconds or until sauce boils.

4. Return pork along with any accumulated juices to wok; heat through. Serve over
rice. *Makes 4 servings*

GINGER BEEF

3 tablespoons soy sauce
2 cloves garlic, minced
1 tablespoon minced fresh ginger
¼ teaspoon crushed red pepper
    flakes
1 beef tenderloin or boneless beef
    sirloin steak, cut 1 inch thick
    (about 1 pound)
¾ cup beef or chicken broth
3½ teaspoons cornstarch

2 tablespoons peanut or vegetable
    oil, divided
1 large yellow onion or sweet
    onion, cut into thin wedges
½ teaspoon sugar
    Hot cooked white rice (optional)
¼ cup coarsely chopped cilantro or
    sliced green onions for
    garnish

1. Combine soy sauce, garlic, ginger and crushed red pepper in medium bowl. Cut
beef across the grain into ⅛-inch slices; cut each slice into 1½-inch pieces. Toss beef
with soy sauce mixture. Marinate at room temperature 20 minutes or cover and
refrigerate up to 4 hours.

2. Blend broth into cornstarch in cup until smooth.

3. Heat wok or large skillet over medium heat. Add 1 tablespoon oil; heat until hot.
Add onion; stir-fry 5 minutes. Sprinkle sugar over onion; cook 5 minutes more or until
onion is light golden brown, stirring occasionally. Remove and reserve.

4. Heat remaining 1 tablespoon oil in wok over medium-high heat until hot. Drain
beef; reserve marinade. Add beef to wok; stir-fry until beef is barely pink in center.
Return onion to wok. Stir broth mixture and add to wok along with reserved marinade.
Stir-fry 1 minute or until sauce boils and thickens. Serve over rice. Garnish with
cilantro. *Makes 4 servings*

BEEF WITH OYSTER SAUCE

Oyster sauce is made with dried oysters, soy sauce and brine. It is used to enhance the flavor of stir-fries.

1 tablespoon soy sauce
2 cloves garlic, minced
¼ to ½ teaspoon crushed red pepper flakes
1 boneless beef top sirloin or tenderloin steak, cut 1 inch thick (about 1 pound)
½ cup chicken broth
¼ cup oyster sauce

1 tablespoon cornstarch
1 tablespoon peanut or vegetable oil
3 thin green onions, cut diagonally into 1-inch pieces
1 teaspoon sesame seeds for garnish (optional)
Hot cooked white rice (optional)

1. Combine soy sauce, garlic and crushed red pepper in medium bowl. Cut beef across the grain into ¼-inch slices; cut each slice into 2-inch pieces. Toss beef with soy sauce mixture. Marinate at room temperature 20 minutes or cover and refrigerate up to 8 hours.

2. Blend broth and oyster sauce into cornstarch in cup until smooth.

3. Heat wok or large skillet over medium-high heat. Add oil; heat until hot. Add half of beef mixture; stir-fry until beef is barely pink in center. Remove and reserve. Repeat with remaining beef mixture; remove and reserve.

4. Stir broth mixture and add to wok along with onions. Stir-fry 1 minute or until sauce boils and thickens.

5. Return beef along with any accumulated juices to wok; heat through. Garnish with sesame seeds. Serve with rice.   *Makes 4 servings*

LEMON-ORANGE GLAZED RIBS

2 whole slabs baby back pork ribs, cut into halves (about 3 pounds)
2 tablespoons soy sauce
2 tablespoons orange juice

2 tablespoons fresh lemon juice
2 cloves garlic, minced
¼ cup orange marmalade
1 tablespoon hoisin sauce

1. Place ribs in large plastic bag. Combine soy sauce, orange and lemon juices and garlic in small bowl; pour over ribs. Close bag securely; turn to coat. Marinate in refrigerator at least 4 hours or up to 24 hours, turning once.

2. Preheat oven to 350°F. Drain ribs; reserve marinade. Place ribs on rack in shallow, foil-lined roasting pan. Brush half of marinade evenly over ribs; bake 20 minutes. Turn ribs over; brush with remaining marinade. Bake 20 minutes.

3. Remove ribs from oven; pour off drippings. Combine marmalade and hoisin sauce in cup; brush half of mixture over ribs. Return to oven; bake 10 minutes or until glazed. Turn ribs over; brush with remaining marmalade mixture. Bake 10 minutes more or until ribs are browned and glazed.   *Makes 4 servings*

CANTON PORK STEW

1½ pounds lean pork shoulder or
    pork loin roast, cut into 1-inch
    pieces
1 teaspoon ground ginger
¼ teaspoon ground cinnamon
¼ teaspoon ground red pepper
1 tablespoon peanut or vegetable
    oil
1 large onion, coarsely chopped
3 cloves garlic, minced

1 can (about 14 ounces) chicken
    broth
¼ cup dry sherry
1 package (about 10 ounces)
    frozen baby carrots, thawed
1 large green bell pepper, cut into
    1-inch pieces
3 tablespoons soy sauce
1½ tablespoons cornstarch
    Cilantro for garnish

1. Sprinkle pork with ginger, cinnamon and ground red pepper; toss well. Heat large saucepan or Dutch oven over medium-high heat. Add oil; heat until hot.

2. Add pork to saucepan; brown on all sides. Add onion and garlic; cook 2 minutes, stirring frequently. Add broth and sherry. Bring to a boil over high heat. Reduce heat to medium-low. Cover and simmer 40 minutes.

3. Stir in carrots and green pepper; cover and simmer 10 minutes or until pork is fork tender. Blend soy sauce into cornstarch in cup until smooth. Stir into stew. Cook and stir 1 minute or until stew boils and thickens. Ladle into soup bowls. Garnish with cilantro.   *Makes 6 servings*

MEAT PATTIES WITH CHINESE GRAVY

1 pound lean ground beef
¼ cup fresh bread crumbs
3 tablespoons minced onion
3 tablespoons chopped cilantro,
    divided
2 tablespoons oyster sauce
2 cloves garlic, minced

1 cup beef broth
1 tablespoon cornstarch
¼ teaspoon sugar
¼ teaspoon crushed red pepper
    flakes (optional)
    Hot cooked white rice (optional)

1. Combine ground beef, bread crumbs, onion, 2 tablespoons cilantro, oyster sauce and garlic in medium bowl. Mix lightly, but thoroughly. Shape to form 4 oval patties, ½ inch thick.

2. Heat large nonstick skillet over medium heat. Add patties; cook 7 minutes. Turn patties over; cook 6 to 7 minutes.*

3. Remove patties to warm serving platter. Spoon off fat from skillet, if necessary. Blend broth into cornstarch in small bowl until smooth. Pour into skillet along with sugar and crushed red pepper. Cook and stir 1 minute or until sauce boils and thickens; pour over patties. Sprinkle with remaining 1 tablespoon cilantro. Serve with rice.   *Makes 4 servings*

*Cooking time is for medium doneness. Adjust time for desired doneness.

Canton Pork Stew

BEEF WITH LEEKS AND TOFU

Tofu is high in protein and allows you to cut back on the amount of beef needed for this recipe.

8 ounces boneless beef sirloin, top loin or tenderloin steak, cut 1 inch thick
2 cloves garlic, minced
8 ounces firm tofu, drained
¾ cup chicken broth
¼ cup soy sauce
1 tablespoon dry sherry
1 tablespoon cornstarch

4 teaspoons peanut or vegetable oil, divided
1 large *or* 2 medium leeks, sliced (white and light green portion)
1 large red bell pepper, cut into short, thin strips
1 tablespoon Oriental sesame oil (optional)
Hot cooked spaghetti (optional)

1. Cut beef across the grain into ⅛-inch slices; cut each slice into 2-inch pieces. Toss beef with garlic in medium bowl. Press tofu lightly between paper towels; cut into ¾-inch triangles or squares.

2. Blend broth, soy sauce and sherry into cornstarch in small bowl until smooth.

3. Heat large, deep skillet over medium-high heat. Add 2 teaspoons peanut oil; heat until hot. Add beef mixture; stir-fry 2 to 2½ minutes until beef is barely pink in center. Remove and reserve.

4. Add remaining 2 teaspoons peanut oil to skillet. Add leek and red pepper; stir-fry 3 minutes or until red pepper is crisp-tender. Stir broth mixture and add to skillet along with tofu. Stir-fry 2 minutes or until sauce boils and thickens and tofu is hot, stirring frequently.

5. Return beef along with any accumulated juices to skillet; heat through. Stir in sesame oil. Serve over spaghetti.   *Makes 4 servings*

Note: For information on storing unused tofu, see page 7.

SPICY GRILLED PORK CHOPS

¼ cup minced onion
¼ cup soy sauce
2 tablespoons fresh lime juice
2 cloves garlic, minced
½ teaspoon crushed red pepper flakes

4 center cut well-trimmed pork loin or rib chops, cut ¾ inch thick

1. Combine onion, soy sauce, lime juice, garlic and crushed red pepper in large plastic bag; add chops. Close bag securely; turn to coat. Marinate in refrigerator at least 4 hours or up to 24 hours, turning once.

2. Drain chops; reserve marinade. Brush with some of the reserved marinade. Grill or broil chops 5 to 6 inches from heat 7 minutes. Turn chops over; brush with marinade, discarding remaining marinade. Grill or broil 8 to 13 minutes until no longer pink.
Makes 4 servings

Beef with Leeks and Tofu

SWEET AND SOUR PORK

To lighten this dish, the pork is stir-fried, not deep-fat fried.

1 tablespoon soy sauce
2 cloves garlic, minced
1 lean boneless pork loin or tenderloin roast* (about 1 pound)
1 can (8 ounces) pineapple chunks in juice, undrained
2 tablespoons peanut or vegetable oil, divided

2 medium carrots, diagonally cut into thin slices
1 large green bell pepper, cut into 1-inch pieces
⅓ cup stir-fry sauce
1 tablespoon white wine or white vinegar
Hot cooked white rice (optional)

1. Combine soy sauce and garlic in medium bowl. Cut pork across the grain into 1-inch pieces; toss with soy sauce mixture.

2. Drain pineapple; reserve 2 tablespoons juice.

3. Heat wok or large skillet over medium-high heat. Add 1 tablespoon oil; heat until hot. Add pork mixture; stir-fry 4 to 5 minutes until pork is no longer pink. Remove and reserve.

4. Heat remaining 1 tablespoon oil in wok. Add carrots and green pepper; stir-fry 4 to 5 minutes until vegetables are crisp-tender. Add pineapple; heat through.

5. Add stir-fry sauce, reserved pineapple juice and vinegar; stir-fry 30 seconds or until sauce boils.

6. Return pork along with any accumulated juices to wok; heat through. Serve over rice.

Makes 4 servings

*Or, substitute 1 pound boneless skinless chicken breasts or thighs.

SESAME-GARLIC FLANK STEAK

1 beef flank steak (about 1¼ pounds)
2 tablespoons soy sauce

2 tablespoons hoisin sauce
1 tablespoon Oriental sesame oil
2 cloves garlic, minced

1. Score steak lightly with a sharp knife in a diamond pattern on both sides; place in large plastic bag.

2. Combine remaining ingredients in small bowl; pour over steak. Close bag securely; turn to coat. Marinate in refrigerator at least 2 hours or up to 24 hours, turning once.

3. Drain steak; reserve marinade. Brush steak with some of the marinade. Grill or broil 5 to 6 inches from heat 5 minutes. Brush with marinade; turn steak over. Discard remaining marinade. Grill or broil 5 to 7 minutes until internal temperature reaches 135°F on meat thermometer inserted in thickest part of steak.*

4. Transfer steak to cutting board; carve across the grain into thin slices.

Makes 4 servings

*Broiling time is for medium-rare doneness. Adjust time for desired doneness.

ORIENTAL BEEF WITH VEGETABLES

*Start with one pound of ground meat to make this easy stir-fry
your kids will love.*

1 pound lean ground beef or
    ground turkey
1 large onion, coarsely chopped
2 cloves garlic, minced
2½ cups (8 ounces) frozen mixed
    vegetable medley, such as
    carrots, broccoli and red
    peppers, thawed

½ cup stir-fry sauce
1 can (3 ounces) chow mein
    noodles

1. Cook beef and onion in wok or large skillet over medium heat until beef is no longer pink, stirring to separate beef. Spoon off fat.

2. Add garlic; stir-fry 1 minute. Add vegetables; stir-fry 2 minutes or until heated through.

3. Add stir-fry sauce; stir-fry 30 seconds or until hot. Serve over chow mein noodles.

Makes 4 servings

ROASTED PORK

3 tablespoons hoisin sauce
1 tablespoon soy sauce
1 tablespoon dry sherry
2 cloves garlic, minced
½ teaspoon crushed Szechuan
    peppercorns or crushed red
    pepper flakes

2 whole pork tenderloin roasts
    (about 1¼ to 1½ pounds total
    weight)

1. Preheat oven to 350°F. Combine hoisin sauce, soy sauce, sherry, garlic and peppercorns in small bowl.

2. Brush one fourth of hoisin sauce mixture evenly over each roast. Place roasts on rack in shallow, foil-lined roasting pan. Cook roasts 15 minutes; turn and brush with remaining hoisin sauce mixture. Continue to cook until internal temperature reaches 155°F on meat thermometer inserted in thickest part of pork. (Timing will depend on thickness of pork; test at 30 minutes.)

3. Let pork stand, tented with foil, on cutting board 5 minutes. (Temperature of pork will rise to 160°F). Slice diagonally and serve warm. Or, for use in other recipes, cut into portions and refrigerate up to 3 days or freeze up to 3 months.

Makes 4 to 6 servings

Variation: For *Chinese Barbecued Pork*, add 1 teaspoon red food coloring to hoisin sauce mixture. Prepare roasts as directed in recipe. Roasts may be grilled over medium coals until an internal temperature reaches 155°F on meat thermometer. (Turn pork after 8 minutes; check temperature at 16 minutes.)

POULTRY

ALMOND CHICKEN

⅓ cup blanched whole almonds
1 pound boneless skinless chicken
   breasts or thighs
2 cloves garlic, minced
1 teaspoon minced fresh ginger
¼ teaspoon crushed red pepper
   flakes
¾ cup chicken broth
¼ cup soy sauce

4 teaspoons cornstarch
4 large ribs bok choy (about
   ¾ pound)
2 tablespoons peanut or vegetable
   oil, divided
2 medium carrots, thinly sliced
   Chow mein noodles or hot
   cooked white rice

1. Preheat oven to 350°F. Spread almonds on baking sheet. Toast 6 to 7 minutes until golden brown, stirring once. Set aside.

2. Cut chicken into 1-inch pieces. Toss chicken with garlic, ginger and crushed red pepper in medium bowl. Marinate chicken at room temperature 15 minutes.

3. Blend broth and soy sauce into cornstarch in small bowl until smooth.

4. Cut woody stems from bok choy leaves; slice stems into ½-inch pieces. Cut tops of leaves crosswise into halves.

5. Heat wok or large skillet over medium-high heat. Add 1 tablespoon oil; heat until hot. Add chicken mixture; stir-fry 3 minutes or until chicken is no longer pink. Remove and reserve.

6. Heat remaining 1 tablespoon oil in wok; add bok choy stems and carrots. Stir-fry 5 minutes or until vegetables are crisp-tender. Stir broth mixture and add to wok along with bok choy leaves. Stir-fry 1 minute or until sauce boils and thickens.

7. Return chicken along with any accumulated juices to wok; heat through. Stir in almonds. Serve over chow mein noodles.

Makes 4 servings

Almond Chicken

GINGERED CHICKEN THIGHS

1 tablespoon peanut or vegetable
   oil
½ teaspoon hot chili oil
8 chicken thighs (1½ to 2 pounds)
2 cloves garlic, minced

¼ cup sweet and sour sauce
1 tablespoon soy sauce
2 teaspoons minced fresh ginger
Cilantro and strips of orange
   peel for garnish

1. Heat large nonstick skillet over medium-high heat. Add peanut oil and chili oil; heat until hot. Cook chicken, skin side down, 4 minutes or until golden brown.

2. Reduce heat to low; turn chicken skin side up. Cover and cook 15 to 18 minutes until juices run clear.

3. Spoon off fat. Increase heat to medium. Stir in garlic and cook 2 minutes. Combine sweet and sour sauce, soy sauce and ginger. Brush half of mixture over chicken; turn chicken over. Brush remaining mixture over chicken. Cook 5 minutes, turning once more, until sauce has thickened and chicken is browned. Transfer chicken to serving platter; pour sauce evenly over chicken. Garnish with cilantro and orange peel.

Makes 4 servings

PINEAPPLE-HOISIN HENS

Hoisin sauce is a sweet-spicy, thick, brown sauce that is frequently used in Chinese cooking.

2 cloves garlic
1 can (8 ounces) crushed
   pineapple in juice, undrained
2 tablespoons rice vinegar
2 tablespoons soy sauce
2 tablespoons hoisin sauce

2 teaspoons minced fresh ginger
1 teaspoon Chinese five-spice
   powder
2 large Cornish hens (about 1½
   pounds each), split in half

1. Mince garlic in blender or food processor. Add pineapple with juice; process until fairly smooth. Add remaining ingredients except hens; process 5 seconds.

2. Place hens in large plastic bag; pour pineapple mixture over hens. Close bag securely; turn to coat. Marinate in refrigerator at least 2 hours or up to 24 hours, turning bag once.

3. Preheat oven to 375°F. Drain hens; reserve marinade. Place hens, skin side up, on rack in shallow, foil-lined roasting pan. Roast 35 minutes.

4. Brush hens lightly with some of the reserved marinade; discard remaining marinade. Roast 10 minutes or until hens are browned and juices run clear.

Makes 4 servings

Gingered Chicken Thighs

SHANGHAI CHICKEN WITH ASPARAGUS AND HAM

2 cups diagonally cut 1-inch
    asparagus pieces*
1 pound boneless skinless chicken
    breasts or thighs
1 tablespoon peanut or vegetable
    oil

1 medium onion, coarsely chopped
2 cloves garlic, minced
¼ cup stir-fry sauce
½ cup diced deli ham
    Hot cooked Chinese egg noodles
    or white rice (optional)

1. To blanch asparagus pieces, cook 3 minutes in boiling water to cover. Plunge asparagus into cold water. Drain well.

2. Cut chicken crosswise into 1-inch pieces.

3. Heat wok or large skillet over medium-high heat. Add oil; heat until hot.

4. Add onion and garlic; stir-fry 2 minutes. Add chicken; stir-fry 2 minutes. Add asparagus; stir-fry 2 minutes or until chicken is no longer pink.

5. Add stir-fry sauce; mix well. Add ham; stir-fry until heated through. Serve over noodles. *Makes 4 servings*

*Or, substitute thawed frozen asparagus. Omit step 1.

CRISPY ROASTED CHICKEN

Any remaining cooked chicken can be used to make another dish, such as Chinese Chicken Salad or Hot and Sour Soup.

1 roasting chicken or capon (about
    6½ pounds)
1 tablespoon peanut or vegetable
    oil

2 cloves garlic, minced
1 tablespoon soy sauce

1. Preheat oven to 350°F. Rinse chicken; pat dry. Place on rack in shallow, foil-lined roasting pan.

2. Combine oil and garlic in small cup; brush evenly over chicken. Roast 15 to 20 minutes per pound or until internal temperature reaches 170°F on meat thermometer inserted in thickest part of thigh.

3. Increase oven temperature to 450°F. Remove drippings from pan; discard. Brush chicken evenly with soy sauce. Roast 5 to 10 minutes until skin is very crisp and deep golden brown. Let stand on cutting board 10 minutes. Cover and refrigerate leftovers up to 3 days or freeze up to 3 months. *Makes 8 to 10 servings*

Shanghai Chicken with Asparagus and Ham

MOO GOO GAI PAN

1 package (1 ounce) dried black
  Chinese mushrooms
¼ cup lite soy sauce
2 tablespoons rice vinegar
3 cloves garlic, minced
1 pound boneless skinless chicken
  breasts
½ cup chicken broth
1 tablespoon cornstarch

2 tablespoons peanut or vegetable
  oil, divided
1 jar (7 ounces) straw mushrooms,
  drained
3 green onions, cut into 1-inch
  pieces
  Hot cooked white rice or Chinese
  egg noodles (optional)

1. Place dried mushrooms in small bowl; cover with warm water. Soak 20 minutes to soften. Drain; squeeze out excess water. Discard stems; slice caps.

2. Combine soy sauce, vinegar and garlic in medium bowl. Cut chicken crosswise into ½-inch strips. Toss chicken with soy sauce mixture. Marinate at room temperature 20 minutes.

3. Blend broth into cornstarch in cup until smooth.

4. Heat wok or large skillet over medium-high heat. Add 1 tablespoon oil; heat until hot. Drain chicken; reserve marinade. Add chicken to wok; stir-fry chicken 3 minutes or until no longer pink. Remove and reserve.

5. Heat remaining 1 tablespoon oil in wok; add dried and straw mushrooms and onions. Stir-fry 1 minute.

6. Stir broth mixture and add to wok along with reserved marinade. Stir-fry 1 minute or until sauce boils and thickens.

7. Return chicken along with any accumulated juices to wok; heat through. Serve over rice.
Makes 4 servings

HONEY-LIME GLAZED CHICKEN

This sweet-sour sauce glazes the chicken beautifully!

1 broiler-fryer chicken, quartered
  (about 3½ pounds) *or* 3
  pounds chicken parts

⅓ cup honey
2 tablespoons fresh lime juice
1½ tablespoons soy sauce

1. Preheat oven to 375°F. Arrange chicken, skin side up, in single layer in shallow casserole dish or 11×7-inch baking dish.

2. Combine remaining ingredients in small bowl; mix well. Brush one third of honey mixture over chicken; bake 15 minutes.

3. Brush one third of honey mixture over chicken; bake 15 minutes. Brush remaining honey mixture over chicken; bake 10 to 15 minutes until juices run clear. Transfer chicken to serving platter. If desired, spoon fat from juices in baking dish; serve with chicken.
Makes 4 servings

SZECHUAN CHICKEN SALAD WITH PEANUT DRESSING

1 pound boneless skinless chicken breast halves
1 can (about 14 ounces) chicken broth
1 tablespoon creamy peanut butter
1 tablespoon peanut or vegetable oil
1 tablespoon soy sauce
1 tablespoon rice vinegar
1 teaspoon Oriental sesame oil
¼ teaspoon ground red pepper
  Shredded lettuce
  Chopped cilantro or green onions (optional)

1. Place chicken in single layer in large skillet. Pour broth over chicken. Bring to a boil over high heat. Reduce heat to medium-low. Cover and simmer 10 to 12 minutes until chicken is no longer pink in center.

2. Meanwhile, mix peanut butter and peanut oil in small bowl until smooth. Stir in soy sauce, rice vinegar, sesame oil and ground red pepper.

3. Drain chicken; reserve broth. Stir 2 tablespoons of the reserved broth* into peanut butter mixture.

4. To serve salad warm, cut chicken crosswise into ½-inch slices and place on lettuce-lined plates. Spoon peanut dressing over chicken. Sprinkle with cilantro.

5. To serve salad at room temperature, cool chicken and shred or coarsely chop. Toss chicken with peanut dressing; cover and refrigerate. Just before serving, bring chicken mixture to room temperature (about 1 hour). Arrange chicken on lettuce-lined plates. Sprinkle with cilantro.   *Makes 4 servings*

*Strain remaining broth; cover and refrigerate or freeze for use in other recipes.

ORIENTAL CHICKEN KABOBS

1 pound boneless skinless chicken breasts
2 small zucchini or yellow squash, cut into 1-inch slices
8 large fresh mushrooms
1 large red, yellow or green bell pepper, cut into 1-inch pieces
¼ cup soy sauce
2 tablespoons dry sherry
2 teaspoons Oriental sesame oil
2 cloves garlic, minced
2 large green onions, cut into 1-inch pieces

1. Cut chicken into 1½-inch pieces; place in large plastic bag. Add zucchini, mushrooms and red pepper to bag. Combine soy sauce, sherry, sesame oil and garlic in cup; pour over chicken and vegetables. Close bag securely; turn to coat. Marinate in refrigerator at least 30 minutes or up to 4 hours.

2. Drain chicken and vegetables; reserve marinade. Alternately thread chicken and vegetables with onions onto metal skewers.

3. Place kabobs on rack of broiler pan. Brush with half of reserved marinade. Broil 5 to 6 inches from heat 5 minutes. Turn kabobs over; brush with remaining marinade. Discard any remaining marinade. Broil 5 minutes or until chicken is no longer pink.
                                                              Makes 4 servings

CHINESE CHICKEN SALAD

This piquant main-dish salad will be a hit with your family.

3 tablespoons peanut or vegetable oil
3 tablespoons rice vinegar
2 tablespoons soy sauce
1 tablespoon honey
1 teaspoon minced fresh ginger
1 teaspoon Oriental sesame oil
1 clove garlic, minced
¼ teaspoon crushed red pepper flakes (optional)
4 cups chopped cooked chicken or turkey

4 cups packed shredded napa cabbage or romaine lettuce
1 cup shredded carrots
½ cup thinly sliced green onions
1 can (5 ounces) chow mein noodles (optional)
¼ cup chopped cashews or peanuts (optional)
Carrot curls and green onions for garnish

1. For dressing, combine peanut oil, vinegar, soy sauce, honey, ginger, sesame oil, garlic and crushed red pepper in small jar with tight-fitting lid; shake well.

2. Place chicken in large bowl. Pour dressing over chicken; toss to coat.*

3. Add cabbage, shredded carrots and sliced onions to bowl; toss well to coat. Serve over chow mein noodles. Sprinkle cashews over salad. Garnish with carrot curls and onions.   *Makes 4 to 6 servings (about 8 cups salad)*

*Salad may be made ahead to this point; cover and refrigerate chicken mixture until ready to serve.

CILANTRO-STUFFED CHICKEN BREASTS

2 cloves garlic
1 cup packed cilantro leaves
1 tablespoon *plus* 2 teaspoons soy sauce, divided
1 tablespoon peanut or vegetable oil

4 chicken breast halves (about 1¼ pounds)
1 tablespoon Oriental sesame oil

1. Preheat oven to 350°F. Mince garlic in blender or food processor. Add cilantro; process until cilantro is minced. Add 2 teaspoons soy sauce and peanut oil; process until paste forms.

2. With rubber spatula or fingers, distribute about 1 tablespoon cilantro mixture evenly under skin of each chicken breast half, taking care not to puncture skin.

3. Place chicken on rack in shallow, foil-lined baking pan. Combine remaining 1 tablespoon soy sauce and sesame oil. Brush half of mixture evenly over chicken. Bake 25 minutes; brush remaining soy sauce mixture evenly over chicken. Bake 10 minutes or until juices run clear.   *Makes 4 servings*

Chinese Chicken Salad

CHINESE CHICKEN STEW

1 package (1 ounce) dried black
  Chinese mushrooms
1 pound boneless skinless chicken
  thighs
1 teaspoon Chinese five-spice
  powder
¼ to ½ teaspoon crushed red
  pepper flakes
1 tablespoon peanut or vegetable
  oil
1 large onion, coarsely chopped
2 cloves garlic, minced
1 can (about 14 ounces) chicken
  broth, divided

1 tablespoon cornstarch
1 large red bell pepper, cut into
  ¾-inch pieces
1 tablespoon soy sauce
2 large green onions, cut into
  ½-inch pieces
1 tablespoon Oriental sesame oil
3 cups hot cooked white rice
  (optional)
¼ cup coarsely chopped cilantro
  (optional)

1. Place mushrooms in small bowl; cover with warm water. Soak 20 minutes to soften. Drain; squeeze out excess water. Discard stems; slice caps.

2. Cut chicken into 1-inch pieces. Toss chicken with five-spice powder in small bowl. Season to taste with crushed red pepper.

3. Heat wok or large skillet over medium-high heat. Add peanut oil; heat until hot. Add chicken mixture, chopped onion and garlic; stir-fry 2 minutes or until chicken is no longer pink.

4. Blend ¼ cup broth into cornstarch in cup until smooth.

5. Add remaining broth to wok. Stir red bell pepper, mushrooms and soy sauce into stew. Reduce heat to medium. Cover and simmer 10 minutes.

6. Stir cornstarch mixture and add to wok. Cook and stir 2 minutes or until sauce boils and thickens. Stir in green onions and sesame oil. Ladle into soup bowls; scoop ½ cup rice into each bowl. Sprinkle with cilantro.   *Makes 6 servings (about 5 cups)*

GARLICKY BAKED CHICKEN

1½ cups fresh bread crumbs
3 cloves garlic, minced
1 tablespoon peanut or vegetable
  oil
2 tablespoons soy sauce

1 tablespoon Chinese hot mustard
1 broiler-fryer chicken, cut up
  (about 3½ pounds) *or*
  3½ pounds chicken parts,
  skinned, if desired

1. Preheat oven to 350°F. Combine bread crumbs, garlic and oil in shallow dish.

2. Combine soy sauce and hot mustard in small bowl; brush evenly over chicken. Dip chicken in bread crumb mixture to coat lightly, but evenly. Place on foil-lined baking sheet.

3. Bake chicken 45 to 55 minutes until juices run clear.   *Makes 4 to 6 servings*

Chinese Chicken Stew

ORANGE-GINGER BROILED CORNISH HENS

This easy-to-do entrée will impress your guests!

**2 large Cornish hens, split (about
1½ pounds each)
2 teaspoons peanut or vegetable
oil, divided**

**¼ cup orange marmalade
1 tablespoon minced fresh ginger**

1. Place hens, skin side up, on rack of foil-lined broiler pan. Brush with 1 teaspoon oil.

2. Broil 6 to 7 inches from heat 10 minutes. Turn hens skin side down; brush with remaining 1 teaspoon oil. Broil 10 minutes.

3. Combine marmalade and ginger in cup; brush half of mixture over hens. Broil 5 minutes.

4. Turn hens skin side up; brush with remaining marmalade mixture. Broil 5 minutes or until juices run clear and hens are browned and glazed.   *Makes 4 servings*

CHICKEN CHOP SUEY

Chop Suey originated in California and literally means "chopped up" leftovers.

**1 package (1 ounce) dried black
Chinese mushrooms
3 tablespoons soy sauce
1 tablespoon cornstarch
1 pound boneless skinless chicken
breasts or thighs
2 cloves garlic, minced
1 tablespoon peanut or vegetable
oil**

**½ cup thinly sliced celery
½ cup sliced water chestnuts
½ cup bamboo shoots
1 cup chicken broth
Hot cooked white rice or chow
mein noodles
Thinly sliced green onions
(optional)**

1. Place mushrooms in small bowl; cover with warm water. Soak 20 minutes to soften. Drain; squeeze out excess water. Discard stems; quarter caps.

2. Blend soy sauce into cornstarch in cup until smooth.

3. Cut chicken into 1-inch pieces; toss with garlic in small bowl. Heat wok or large skillet over medium-high heat. Add oil; heat until hot. Add chicken mixture and celery; stir-fry 2 minutes. Add water chestnuts and bamboo shoots; stir-fry 1 minute. Add broth and mushrooms; cook 3 minutes or until chicken is no longer pink in center, stirring frequently.

4. Stir soy sauce mixture and add to wok. Cook and stir 1 to 2 minutes until sauce boils and thickens. Serve over rice. Garnish with onions.   *Makes 4 servings*

Note: For information on storing unused bamboo shoots and water chestnuts, see pages 6 and 7.

Orange-Ginger Broiled Cornish Hen

CHICKEN CHOW MEIN

This light version of chow mein omits the deep-fat frying of the noodles.

1 pound boneless skinless chicken
   breasts or thighs
2 cloves garlic, minced
2 tablespoons peanut or vegetable
   oil, divided
¼ cup soy sauce
2 tablespoons dry sherry
6 ounces (2 cups) fresh snow peas
   or 1 package (6 ounces) frozen
   snow peas, thawed, cut into
   halves

3 large green onions, cut
   diagonally into 1-inch pieces
6 ounces uncooked Chinese egg
   noodles or vermicelli, cooked,
   drained and rinsed
1 tablespoon Oriental sesame oil

1. Cut chicken crosswise into ¼-inch slices; cut each slice into 1 × ¼-inch strips. Toss chicken with garlic in small bowl.

2. Heat wok or large skillet over medium-high heat. Add 1 tablespoon peanut oil; heat until hot. Add chicken mixture; stir-fry 3 minutes or until chicken is no longer pink. Transfer to bowl; toss with soy sauce and sherry.

3. Heat remaining 1 tablespoon peanut oil in wok. Add snow peas; stir-fry 2 minutes for fresh or 1 minute for frozen snow peas. Add onions; stir-fry 30 seconds. Add chicken mixture; stir-fry 1 minute.

4. Add noodles to wok; stir-fry 2 minutes or until heated through. Stir in sesame oil; serve immediately.   *Makes 4 servings*

HOISIN-ROASTED CHICKEN WITH VEGETABLES

1 broiler-fryer chicken, cut up
   (about 3 pounds)
3 tablespoons hoisin sauce
1 tablespoon dry sherry
1 tablespoon Oriental sesame oil
6 ounces medium or large fresh
   mushrooms

2 small red or yellow onions, cut
   into thin wedges
1 package (9 or 10 ounces) frozen
   baby carrots, thawed

1. Preheat oven to 375°F. Place chicken, skin side up, in shallow, lightly oiled, foil-lined roasting pan.

2. Combine hoisin sauce, sherry and sesame oil in small bowl. Brush half of mixture evenly over chicken; bake 20 minutes.

3. Scatter mushrooms, onions and carrots around chicken. Brush remaining hoisin sauce mixture over chicken and vegetables; bake 20 minutes or until juices from chicken run clear.   *Makes 4 to 6 servings*

Chicken Chow Mein

SESAME CHICKEN

1 pound boneless skinless chicken breasts or thighs	2 cloves garlic, minced
⅓ cup teriyaki sauce	2 large green onions, cut into ½-inch slices
2 teaspoons cornstarch	1 tablespoon toasted sesame seeds*
1 tablespoon peanut or vegetable oil	1 teaspoon Oriental sesame oil

1. Cut chicken into 1-inch pieces; toss chicken with teriyaki sauce in small bowl. Marinate at room temperature 15 minutes or cover and refrigerate up to 2 hours.

2. Drain chicken; reserve marinade. Blend reserved marinade into cornstarch in cup until smooth.

3. Heat wok or large skillet over medium-high heat. Add peanut oil; heat until hot. Add chicken and garlic; stir-fry 3 minutes or until chicken is no longer pink. Stir marinade mixture and add to wok along with onions and sesame seeds. Stir-fry 30 seconds or until sauce boils and thickens. Stir in sesame oil.   *Makes 4 servings*

*To toast sesame seeds, spread seeds in small skillet. Shake skillet over medium heat 2 minutes or until seeds begin to pop and turn golden.

CHINESE CURRIED CHICKEN

Coconut milk is available in cans in the ethnic food section of large supermarkets. If you prefer, substitute chicken broth for the coconut milk.

1 pound boneless skinless chicken breasts or thighs	3 tablespoons soy sauce
1 tablespoon all-purpose flour	6 ounces (2 cups) fresh snow peas *or* 1 package (6 ounces) frozen snow peas, thawed
1 tablespoon curry powder	Hot cooked white rice or Chinese egg noodles
¼ teaspoon salt	
¼ teaspoon ground red pepper	¼ cup chopped cilantro or thinly sliced green onions
2 tablespoons peanut or vegetable oil, divided	2 tablespoons chopped peanuts or cashews
1 large onion, chopped	
2 cloves garlic, minced	
1 can (14 ounces) coconut milk	

1. Cut chicken into 1-inch pieces. Combine flour, curry powder, salt and ground red pepper in medium plastic bag. Add chicken; shake to coat.

2. Heat large skillet over medium-high heat. Add 1 tablespoon oil; heat until hot. Add onion and garlic; cook 3 minutes, stirring occasionally.

3. Push onion mixture to edges of skillet. Add remaining 1 tablespoon oil and chicken mixture; stir-fry 2 to 3 minutes until chicken is no longer pink. Add coconut milk and soy sauce; reduce heat to medium-low. Simmer, uncovered, 10 minutes.

4. Stir in snow peas; cook 4 minutes for fresh or 2 minutes for frozen snow peas or until crisp-tender and sauce is slightly thickened. Serve over rice. Sprinkle with cilantro and peanuts.   *Makes 4 servings*

KUNG PO CHICKEN

Kung Po Chicken is a Szechuan specialty. This version uses hot chili oil for the heat and is milder than recipes using dried chilies.

1 pound boneless skinless chicken breasts or thighs
2 cloves garlic, minced
1 teaspoon hot chili oil
¼ cup lite soy sauce
2 teaspoons cornstarch
1 tablespoon peanut or vegetable oil

⅓ cup roasted peanuts
2 green onions, cut into short, thin strips
Lettuce leaves (optional)
Plum sauce (optional)

1. Cut chicken into 1-inch pieces. Toss chicken with garlic and chili oil in medium bowl.

2. Blend soy sauce into cornstarch in cup until smooth.

3. Heat wok or large skillet over medium-high heat. Add peanut oil; heat until hot. Add chicken mixture; stir-fry 3 minutes or until chicken is no longer pink.

4. Stir soy sauce mixture and add to wok along with peanuts and onions. Stir-fry 1 minute or until sauce boils and thickens.

5. To serve, spread each lettuce leaf lightly with plum sauce. Add chicken mixture; roll up and serve immediately. *Makes 4 main-dish or 8 appetizer servings*

CASHEW CHICKEN

1 pound boneless skinless chicken breasts or thighs
2 teaspoons minced fresh ginger
1 tablespoon peanut or vegetable oil
1 medium red bell pepper, cut into short, thin strips

⅓ cup teriyaki baste and glaze sauce
⅓ cup roasted or dry roasted cashews
Hot cooked white rice (optional)
Coarsely chopped cilantro (optional)

1. Cut chicken into ½-inch slices; cut each slice into 1½×½-inch strips. Toss chicken with ginger in small bowl.

2. Heat wok or large skillet over medium-high heat. Add oil; heat until hot. Add chicken mixture; stir-fry 2 minutes. Add red pepper; stir-fry 4 minutes or until chicken is no longer pink and red pepper is crisp-tender.

3. Add teriyaki sauce; stir-fry 1 minute or until sauce is hot. Stir in cashews. Serve over rice. Sprinkle with cilantro. *Makes 4 servings*

SEAFOOD

EASY SEAFOOD STIR-FRY

Dried black mushrooms must be soaked before using.
They add a unique flavor to dishes.

1 package (1 ounce) dried black
    Chinese mushrooms*
1 cup chicken broth
3 tablespoons soy sauce
2 tablespoons dry sherry
4½ teaspoons cornstarch
2 tablespoons peanut or vegetable
    oil, divided
½ pound medium raw shrimp,
    peeled, deveined

½ pound bay scallops or halved
    sea scallops
2 cloves garlic, minced
6 ounces (2 cups) fresh snow peas,
    cut diagonally into halves
Sesame Noodle Cake (page 78)
    or hot cooked white rice
    (optional)
¼ cup thinly sliced green onions
    (optional)

1. Place mushrooms in small bowl; cover with warm water. Soak 20 minutes to soften. Drain; squeeze out excess water. Discard stems; slice caps.

2. Blend broth, soy sauce and sherry into cornstarch in another small bowl until smooth.

3. Heat wok or large skillet over medium-high heat. Add 1 tablespoon oil; heat until hot. Add shrimp, scallops and garlic; stir-fry 3 minutes or until seafood is opaque. Remove and reserve.

4. Add remaining 1 tablespoon oil to wok. Add mushrooms and snow peas; stir-fry 3 minutes or until snow peas are crisp-tender.

5. Stir broth mixture and add to wok. Stir-fry 2 minutes or until sauce boils and thickens.

6. Return seafood along with any accumulated juices to wok; heat through. Serve over Sesame Noodle Cake. Garnish with onions.   *Makes 4 servings*

*Or, substitute 1½ cups sliced fresh mushrooms. Omit step 1.

Easy Seafood Stir-Fry served over Sesame
Noodle Cake (page 78)

GRILLED CHINESE SALMON

While salmon is not a traditional Chinese fish, this recipe gives it an Oriental twist.

3 tablespoons soy sauce
2 tablespoons dry sherry
2 cloves garlic, minced

1 pound salmon steaks or fillets
2 tablespoons finely chopped
   fresh cilantro

1. Combine soy sauce, sherry and garlic in shallow dish. Add salmon; turn to coat. Cover and refrigerate at least 30 minutes or up to 2 hours.

2. Drain salmon; reserve marinade. Arrange steaks (arrange fillets skin side down) on oiled rack of broiler pan or oiled grid over hot coals. Broil or grill 5 to 6 inches from heat 10 minutes. Baste with reserved marinade after 5 minutes of broiling; discard any remaining marinade. Sprinkle with cilantro.   *Makes 4 servings*

STIR-FRIED CRAB

For best results use firm to extra-firm tofu for stir-fries and gently stir tofu into dish.

8 ounces firm tofu, drained
1 tablespoon soy sauce
¼ cup chicken broth
3 tablespoons oyster sauce
2 teaspoons cornstarch
1 tablespoon peanut or vegetable
   oil
6 ounces (2 cups) fresh snow peas,
   cut into halves *or* 1 package
   (6 ounces) frozen snow peas,
   separated, but not thawed

8 ounces thawed frozen cooked
   crabmeat or imitation
   crabmeat, broken into ½-inch
   pieces (about 2 cups)
Sesame Noodle Cake (page 78)
   (optional)
2 tablespoons chopped cilantro or
   thinly sliced green onions

1. Press tofu lightly between paper towels; cut into ½-inch squares or triangles. Place in shallow dish. Drizzle soy sauce over tofu.

2. Blend broth and oyster sauce into cornstarch in cup until smooth.

3. Heat wok or large skillet over medium-high heat. Add oil; heat until hot. Add snow peas; stir-fry 3 minutes for fresh or 2 minutes for frozen snow peas. Add crabmeat; stir-fry 1 minute. Stir broth mixture and add to wok. Stir-fry 30 seconds or until sauce boils and thickens.

4. Stir in tofu mixture; heat through. Serve over Sesame Noodle Cake. Sprinkle with cilantro.   *Makes 4 servings*

Note: For information on storing unused tofu, see page 7.

Grilled Chinese Salmon

GARLIC SKEWERED SHRIMP

For a prettier presentation, leave the tails on the shrimp.

1 pound large raw shrimp, peeled, deveined
2 tablespoons soy sauce
1 tablespoon peanut or vegetable oil

3 cloves garlic, minced
¼ teaspoon crushed red pepper flakes (optional)
3 green onions, cut into 1-inch pieces

1. Soak 4 (12-inch) bamboo skewers in water to cover 20 minutes.

2. Place shrimp in large plastic bag. Combine soy sauce, oil, garlic and crushed red pepper in cup; mix well. Pour over shrimp. Close bag securely; turn to coat. Marinate at room temperature 10 to 15 minutes.

3. Drain shrimp; reserve marinade. Alternately thread shrimp and onions onto skewers. Place on rack of broiler pan. Brush with reserved marinade; discard remaining marinade.

4. Broil shrimp 5 to 6 inches from heat 5 minutes. Turn shrimp over; broil 5 minutes or until shrimp are opaque. *Makes 4 servings*

SHANGHAI STEAMED FISH

1 cleaned whole sea bass, red snapper, carp or grouper (about 1½ pounds)
¼ cup teriyaki sauce
2 teaspoons shredded fresh ginger

2 green onions, cut into 4-inch pieces
1 teaspoon Oriental sesame oil (optional)

1. Sprinkle inside cavity of fish with teriyaki sauce and ginger. Place onions in cavity in single layer.

2. Pour enough water into wok so that water is just below steaming rack. Bring water to a boil over high heat. Reduce heat to medium-low to maintain a simmer. Place fish on steaming rack in steamer. Cover and steam fish over simmering water about 10 minutes per inch of thickness measured at thickest part of fish. Fish is done when it flakes easily when tested with fork.

3. Carefully remove fish; discard onions. Cut fish into four serving-size portions. Sprinkle with sesame oil. *Makes 4 servings*

Garlic Skewered Shrimp

BEIJING FILLET OF SOLE

These rolled stuffed fillets are easy-to-make and bake in just 30 minutes.

2 tablespoons soy sauce
1 tablespoon Oriental sesame oil
4 sole fillets (6 ounces each)
1¼ cups preshredded coleslaw mix
    or cabbage

½ cup crushed chow mein noodles
1 egg white, slightly beaten
2 teaspoons toasted sesame seeds*

1. Preheat oven to 350°F. Combine soy sauce and sesame oil in small bowl. Place sole in shallow dish. Lightly brush both sides of sole with soy sauce mixture.

2. Combine coleslaw mix, noodles, egg white and remaining soy sauce mixture in small bowl. Spoon evenly over sole. Roll up each fillet and place, seam side down, in shallow, foil-lined roasting pan. Sprinkle rolls with sesame seeds. Bake 25 to 30 minutes until fish flakes easily when tested with fork.   *Makes 4 servings*

*To toast sesame seeds, spread seeds in small skillet. Shake skillet over medium heat 2 minutes or until seeds begin to pop and turn golden.

FIVE-SPICE SHRIMP WITH WALNUTS

1 pound medium or large raw
    shrimp, peeled, deveined
½ teaspoon Chinese five-spice
    powder
2 cloves garlic, minced
½ cup chicken broth
2 tablespoons soy sauce
2 tablespoons dry sherry
1 tablespoon cornstarch

1 tablespoon peanut or vegetable
    oil
1 large red bell pepper, cut into
    short, thin strips
⅓ cup walnut halves or quarters
    Hot cooked white rice (optional)
¼ cup thinly sliced green onions
    (optional)

1. Toss shrimp with five-spice powder and garlic in small bowl.

2. Blend broth, soy sauce and sherry into cornstarch in cup until smooth.

3. Heat wok or large skillet over medium-high heat. Add oil; heat until hot. Add shrimp mixture, red pepper and walnuts; stir-fry 3 to 5 minutes until shrimp are opaque and red pepper is crisp-tender.

4. Stir broth mixture and add to wok. Stir-fry 1 minute or until sauce boils and thickens. Serve over rice. Garnish with onions.   *Makes 4 servings*

Beijing Fillet of Sole

HOT AND SOUR SHRIMP

The crushed red pepper creates the hot and the vinegar creates the sour in this scrumptious shrimp stir-fry.

½ package (½ ounce) dried black
   Chinese mushrooms
½ small unpeeled cucumber
1 tablespoon brown sugar
2 teaspoons cornstarch
3 tablespoons rice vinegar
2 tablespoons soy sauce
1 tablespoon peanut or vegetable
   oil

1 pound medium raw shrimp,
   peeled, deveined
2 cloves garlic, minced
¼ teaspoon crushed red pepper
   flakes
1 large red bell pepper, cut into
   short, thin strips
Hot cooked white rice or Chinese
   egg noodles (optional)

1. Place mushrooms in small bowl; cover with warm water. Soak 20 minutes to soften. Drain; squeeze out excess water. Discard stems; slice caps.

2. Cut cucumber in half lengthwise; scrape out seeds. Slice crosswise.

3. Combine brown sugar and cornstarch in small bowl. Blend in vinegar and soy sauce until smooth.

4. Heat wok or large skillet over medium-high heat. Add oil; heat until hot. Add shrimp, garlic and crushed red pepper; stir-fry 1 minute. Add mushrooms and red pepper strips; stir-fry 2 minutes or until shrimp are opaque.

5. Stir vinegar mixture and add to wok. Stir-fry 30 seconds or until sauce boils and thickens. Add cucumber; stir-fry until heated through. Serve over rice.

Makes 4 servings

HALIBUT WITH CILANTRO AND LIME

1 pound halibut, tuna or swordfish
   steaks
2 tablespoons fresh lime juice
¼ cup regular or lite teriyaki sauce
1 teaspoon cornstarch
½ teaspoon minced fresh ginger

1 tablespoon peanut or vegetable
   oil
½ cup slivered red or yellow onion
2 cloves garlic, minced
¼ cup coarsely chopped cilantro

1. Cut halibut into 1-inch pieces; sprinkle with lime juice.

2. Blend teriyaki sauce into cornstarch in cup until smooth. Stir in ginger.

3. Heat wok or large skillet over medium-high heat. Add oil; heat until hot. Add onion and garlic; stir-fry 2 minutes. Add halibut; stir-fry 2 minutes or until halibut is opaque.

4. Stir teriyaki sauce mixture and add to wok. Stir-fry 30 seconds or until sauce boils and thickens. Sprinkle with cilantro.

Makes 4 servings

BROILED HUNAN FISH FILLETS

3 tablespoons soy sauce
1 tablespoon finely chopped green
  onion
2 teaspoons Oriental sesame oil
1 teaspoon minced fresh ginger

1 clove garlic, minced
¼ teaspoon crushed red pepper
  flakes
1 pound red snapper, scrod or cod
  fillets

1. Combine soy sauce, onion, sesame oil, ginger, garlic and crushed pepper in cup.

2. Spray rack of broiler pan with nonstick cooking spray. Place fish on rack; brush with soy sauce mixture.

3. Broil 4 to 5 inches from heat 10 minutes or until fish flakes easily when tested with fork. *Makes 4 servings*

ORANGE-ALMOND SCALLOPS

3 tablespoons orange juice
3 tablespoons soy sauce
1 clove garlic, minced
1 pound bay scallops or halved
  sea scallops
1 tablespoon cornstarch
2 tablespoons peanut or vegetable
  oil, divided

1 green bell pepper, cut into short,
  thin strips
1 can (8 ounces) sliced water
  chestnuts, drained and rinsed
⅓ cup toasted blanched almonds
  Hot cooked white rice (optional)
½ teaspoon finely grated orange
  peel

1. Combine orange juice, soy sauce and garlic in medium bowl. Add scallops; toss to coat. Marinate at room temperature 15 minutes or cover and refrigerate up to 1 hour.

2. Drain scallops; reserve marinade. Blend marinade into cornstarch in cup until smooth.

3. Heat wok or large skillet over medium-high heat. Add 1 tablespoon oil; heat until hot. Add scallops; stir-fry 2 minutes or until scallops are opaque. Remove and reserve.

4. Add remaining 1 tablespoon oil to wok. Add green pepper and water chestnuts. Stir-fry 3 minutes.

5. Return scallops along with any accumulated juices to wok. Stir marinade mixture and add to wok. Stir-fry 1 minute or until sauce boils and thickens. Stir in almonds. Serve over rice. Sprinkle with orange peel. *Makes 4 servings*

RICE & NOODLES

RICE NOODLES WITH PEPPERS

3½ ounces dried Chinese rice sticks
  or rice noodles
⅓ cup chicken broth
3 tablespoons soy sauce
2 tablespoons tomato paste
1 tablespoon peanut or vegetable
  oil

1 medium green bell pepper, cut
  into long, thin strips
1 medium red bell pepper, cut into
  long, thin strips
1 medium onion, cut into thin
  wedges
2 cloves garlic, minced

1. Place rice sticks in bowl; cover with warm water. Soak 15 minutes to soften. Drain; cut into 3-inch pieces.

2. Combine broth, soy sauce and tomato paste in cup.

3. Heat wok or large skillet over medium-high heat. Add oil; heat until hot. Add peppers, onion and garlic; stir-fry 4 to 5 minutes until vegetables are crisp-tender.

4. Stir in broth mixture; heat through. Add noodles; stir-fry 3 minutes or until heated through. *Makes 6 servings*

VEGETABLE FRIED RICE

1 tablespoon peanut or vegetable
  oil
1½ cups small broccoli florets
¾ cup chopped red bell pepper
3 cups chilled cooked white rice

2 tablespoons soy sauce
½ cup shredded carrot
½ teaspoon Oriental sesame oil
  (optional)
Purple kale leaves (optional)

1. Heat large nonstick skillet over medium heat. Add peanut oil; heat until hot. Add broccoli and red pepper; stir-fry 3 minutes or until vegetables are crisp-tender.

2. Add rice and soy sauce; stir-fry 2 minutes. Add carrot; heat through. Stir in sesame oil. Serve rice mixture on kale-lined plates. *Makes 4 servings*

*Top to bottom: Rice Noodles with Peppers
and Vegetable Fried Rice*

CELLOPHANE NOODLE SALAD

The terms cellophane noodles and bean threads are used interchangeably. They refer to transparent noodles made from mung beans.

1 package (3¾ ounces) bean threads
2 tablespoons peanut or vegetable oil
8 ounces medium or large raw shrimp, peeled, deveined
3 cloves garlic, minced
¼ teaspoon crushed red pepper flakes

½ cup cooked pork or ham strips (optional)
2 tablespoons soy sauce
1 tablespoon fresh lemon juice
1 tablespoon rice vinegar
1 tablespoon Oriental sesame oil
⅓ cup thinly sliced green onions or coarsely chopped cilantro

1. Place bean threads in medium bowl; cover with warm water. Soak 15 minutes to soften. Drain well; cut into 2-inch pieces.

2. Heat wok or large skillet over medium-high heat. Add peanut oil; heat until hot. Add shrimp, garlic and crushed red pepper; stir-fry 2 minutes. Add pork, soy sauce, lemon juice, vinegar and sesame oil; stir-fry 1 minute.

3. Add bean threads; stir-fry 1 minute or until heated through. Serve warm, chilled or at room temperature. Sprinkle with onions before serving.   *Makes 4 servings*

PORK FRIED RICE

This is a great way to use up leftover rice and pork and make a wonderful meal.

1 egg
1 egg white
1 tablespoon *plus* 2 teaspoons peanut or vegetable oil, divided
3 cups chilled cooked white rice

2 tablespoons stir-fry sauce
1 cup diced cooked pork*
½ cup frozen baby peas or drained canned peas
½ cup thinly sliced green onions

1. Beat egg with egg white in small bowl.

2. Heat large nonstick skillet over medium-high heat. Add 2 teaspoons oil; heat until hot. Add eggs, tilting skillet to coat surface. Cook 2 minutes or until eggs are set and lightly browned on bottom. Transfer to plate.

3. Heat remaining 1 tablespoon oil in skillet. Add rice and stir-fry sauce; mix well. Stir in pork, peas and onions; heat through, stirring frequently.

4. Cut egg pancake into short, thin strips. Gently stir into rice mixture; heat through.
Makes 2 main-dish or 4 side-dish servings

*Or, substitute 1 cup small cooked shrimp, diced cooked beef or chicken for the pork.

SZECHUAN COLD NOODLES

8 ounces vermicelli, broken in half or Chinese egg noodles
3 tablespoons soy sauce
2 tablespoons peanut or vegetable oil
3 tablespoons rice vinegar
1 large clove garlic, minced
1 teaspoon minced fresh ginger

1 teaspoon Oriental sesame oil (optional)
½ teaspoon crushed Szechuan peppercorns or crushed red pepper flakes
½ cup coarsely chopped cilantro (optional)
¼ cup chopped peanuts

1. Cook vermicelli according to package directions; drain.

2. Combine soy sauce, peanut oil, vinegar, garlic, ginger, sesame oil and peppercorns in large bowl. Add hot vermicelli; toss to coat. Sprinkle with cilantro and peanuts. Serve at room temperature or chilled. *Makes 4 servings*

Variation: For *Szechuan Vegetable Noodles*, add 1 cup chopped peeled cucumber, ½ cup *each* chopped red bell pepper and sliced green onions and an additional 1 tablespoon soy sauce.

CANTONESE RICE CAKE PATTIES

2 cups chilled cooked white rice
⅓ cup chopped red bell pepper
¼ cup thinly sliced green onions
2 tablespoons soy sauce

2 egg whites, slightly beaten
1 egg, slightly beaten
3 tablespoons peanut or vegetable oil, divided

1. Mix rice, red pepper, onions, soy sauce, egg whites and egg in medium bowl.

2. Heat large nonstick skillet over medium heat. Add 1 tablespoon oil; heat until hot. For each patty, spoon ⅓ cup rice mixture into skillet; flatten patties slightly with back of spatula. Cook patties, 3 at a time, 3 to 4 minutes until bottoms are golden brown. Turn patties over; cook 3 minutes or until golden brown. Keep patties warm in 200°F oven. Repeat with remaining oil and rice mixture.

Makes about 6 servings (about 9 patties)

EGG NOODLES WITH OYSTER SAUCE AND GREEN ONIONS

½ cup beef broth
2 tablespoons oyster sauce
1 tablespoon soy sauce
¼ teaspoon crushed red pepper flakes

6 ounces Chinese egg noodles or vermicelli, hot cooked and drained
2 green onions, cut into short, thin strips
2 teaspoons Oriental sesame oil

1. Heat broth, oyster sauce, soy sauce and crushed red pepper in medium saucepan over medium heat. Add noodles; heat through.

2. Stir in onions and sesame oil. Serve warm, chilled or at room temperature.

Makes 4 servings

ORIENTAL PILAF

1 medium onion, chopped
2 cloves garlic, minced
1 tablespoon peanut or vegetable
   oil
1 cup long-grain white rice
1 can (about 14 ounces) chicken or
   beef broth

¼ cup water*
3 ounces (1 cup) fresh snow peas,
   cut lengthwise into thin strips
2 medium carrots, coarsely
   shredded

1. Cook and stir onion and garlic in oil in medium saucepan over medium heat 4 minutes or until tender. Add rice; cook and stir 1 minute.

2. Add broth and water. Bring to a boil over high heat. Reduce heat to low. Cover and simmer 18 minutes. Stir in snow peas and carrots. Cover and simmer 2 minutes or until liquid is absorbed.

3. Let stand, covered, 5 minutes; fluff with fork before serving.

Makes 4 to 6 servings

*If using converted rice, increase water to ½ cup.

GINGER NOODLES WITH SESAME EGG STRIPS

2 egg whites
1 egg
3 tablespoons soy sauce, divided
3 teaspoons toasted sesame
   seeds,* divided
1 tablespoon peanut or vegetable
   oil

½ cup chicken broth
1 teaspoon minced fresh ginger
1 teaspoon Oriental sesame oil
6 ounces Chinese egg noodles or
   vermicelli, hot cooked and
   well drained
⅓ cup sliced green onions

1. Beat together egg whites, egg, 1 tablespoon soy sauce and 1 teaspoon sesame seeds in small bowl.

2. Heat large nonstick skillet over medium-high heat. Add peanut oil; heat until hot. Pour egg mixture into skillet; cook 1½ to 2 minutes or until bottom of omelet is set. Turn omelet over; cook 30 seconds to 1 minute. Slide out onto plate; cool and cut into ½-inch strips.

3. Add broth, remaining 2 tablespoons soy sauce, ginger and sesame oil to skillet. Bring to a boil; reduce heat. Add noodles; heat through. Add omelet strips and onions; heat through. Sprinkle with remaining 2 teaspoons sesame seeds.

Makes 4 servings

*To toast sesame seeds, spread seeds in small skillet. Shake skillet over medium heat 2 minutes or until seeds begin to pop and turn golden.

SINGAPORE RICE SALAD

1 can (8 ounces) pineapple tidbits
   or chunks in juice, undrained
3 cups chilled cooked white rice
1 cup diced cucumber
1 red bell pepper, diced
½ cup sliced green onions
½ cup shredded carrots
¼ cup peanut or vegetable oil

¼ cup teriyaki sauce
1 tablespoon fresh lime juice
   Chopped fresh cilantro
      (optional)
   Chopped peanuts or cashews
      (optional)
   Cucumber slices for garnish

1. Drain pineapple; reserve 3 tablespoons juice. Combine rice, diced cucumber, red pepper, onions, carrots and pineapple in large bowl.

2. Combine oil, teriyaki sauce, lime juice and reserved pineapple juice in small bowl; mix well. Pour over salad; toss to coat. Cover and refrigerate at least 2 hours or up to 12 hours. Sprinkle with cilantro and peanuts before serving. Garnish with cucumber slices.   *Makes 6 to 8 servings*

VEGETABLE LO MEIN

8 ounces vermicelli, thin spaghetti
   or Chinese mein noodles,
   cooked and drained
1½ tablespoons Oriental sesame oil
2 teaspoons peanut or vegetable
   oil
2 teaspoons minced fresh ginger

2 cups sliced bok choy
1 cup fresh or drained, rinsed
   canned bean sprouts
½ cup chicken broth
2 tablespoons oyster sauce
1 tablespoon soy sauce

1. Toss vermicelli with sesame oil in large bowl to coat well.

2. Heat large nonstick skillet over medium heat. Add peanut oil; heat until hot. Stir in ginger.

3. Add bok choy; stir-fry 3 to 4 minutes or until crisp-tender. Add bean sprouts; stir-fry 1 minute.

4. Stir in broth, oyster sauce and soy sauce; mix well. Add vermicelli mixture; heat through, stirring until liquid is absorbed.   *Makes 6 servings*

Note: For information on storing unused bean sprouts, see page 6.

Singapore Rice Salad

EGG FOO YUNG

*Two egg whites were substituted for one of the whole eggs to
lighten this popular dish.*

2 eggs
2 egg whites
½ cup fresh or drained, rinsed
   canned bean sprouts
½ cup chopped fresh mushrooms
2 tablespoons thinly sliced green
   onion

2 tablespoons soy sauce, divided
1 tablespoon peanut or vegetable
   oil
1 cup chicken broth
1 tablespoon cornstarch
¼ teaspoon sugar
¼ teaspoon black pepper

1. Beat eggs with egg whites in large bowl. Stir in bean sprouts, mushrooms, onion
and 1 tablespoon soy sauce.

2. Heat large nonstick skillet over medium-high heat. Add oil; heat until hot. To form
each pancake, pour ¼ cup egg mixture into skillet (egg mixture will run; do not crowd
skillet). Cook 1 to 2 minutes until bottoms of pancakes are set. Turn pancakes over;
cook 1 to 2 minutes until pancakes are cooked through. Remove and keep warm.
Repeat with remaining egg mixture.

3. Blend broth into cornstarch in small bowl until smooth. Stir into skillet. Stir in sugar
and pepper; cook and stir 1 minute or until sauce boils and thickens.

4. Pour sauce over warm pancakes; serve immediately.

Makes 2 main-dish or 4 side-dish servings

Variation: Add ½ cup chopped cooked shrimp or ½ cup diced roasted pork to egg
mixture.

Note: For information on storing unused bean sprouts, see page 6.

SESAME NOODLE CAKE

*Sesame Noodle Cake may be used in place of rice as a base for entrées,
such as Easy Seafood Stir-Fry, Stir-Fried Crab and Ming Dynasty Beef Stew.*

4 ounces vermicelli or Chinese egg
   noodles
1 tablespoon soy sauce

1 tablespoon peanut or vegetable
   oil
½ teaspoon Oriental sesame oil

1. Cook vermicelli according to package directions; drain well. Place in large bowl.
Toss with soy sauce until sauce is absorbed.

2. Heat 10- or 11-inch nonstick skillet over medium heat. Add peanut oil; heat until
hot. Add vermicelli mixture; pat into an even layer with spatula.

3. Cook, uncovered, 6 minutes or until bottom is lightly browned. Invert onto plate,
then slide back into skillet, browned side up. Cook 4 minutes or until bottom is well-
browned. Drizzle with sesame oil. Transfer to serving platter and cut into quarters.

Makes 4 servings

CURRIED NOODLES

For a spicier noodle dish, use ¼ teaspoon crushed red pepper flakes.

**7 ounces dried Chinese rice sticks
  or rice noodles**
**1 tablespoon peanut or vegetable
  oil**
**1 large red bell pepper, cut into
  short, thin strips**
**2 large green onions, cut into
  ½-inch pieces**

1 clove garlic, minced
1 teaspoon minced fresh ginger
2 teaspoons curry powder
**⅛ to ¼ teaspoon crushed red
  pepper flakes**
½ cup chicken broth
2 tablespoons soy sauce

1. Place rice sticks in bowl; cover with warm water. Soak 15 minutes to soften. Drain; cut into 3-inch pieces.

2. Heat wok or large skillet over medium-high heat. Add oil; heat until hot. Add red pepper strips; stir-fry 3 minutes.

3. Add onions, garlic and ginger; stir-fry 1 minute. Add curry powder and crushed red pepper; stir-fry 1 minute.

4. Add broth and soy sauce; heat through. Add noodles; stir-fry 3 minutes or until heated through. *Makes 6 servings*

BEAN THREADS WITH TOFU AND VEGETABLES

8 ounces firm tofu, drained
4 tablespoons soy sauce, divided
1 tablespoon Oriental sesame oil
**1 can (about 14 ounces) chicken
  broth**
2 tablespoons dry sherry

**1 package (3¾ ounces) bean
  threads**
**2 cups frozen mixed vegetable
  medley, such as broccoli,
  carrot and red pepper, thawed**

1. Press tofu lightly between paper towels; cut into ¾-inch cubes or triangles. Place on shallow plate; drizzle with 1 tablespoon soy sauce and sesame oil.

2. Combine broth, remaining 3 tablespoons soy sauce and sherry in deep skillet or large saucepan. Bring to a boil; reduce heat. Add bean threads; simmer, uncovered, 7 minutes or until noodles absorb liquid, stirring occasionally to separate noodles.

3. Stir in vegetables; heat through. Stir in tofu mixture; cover and heat through, about 1 minute. *Makes 6 servings*

Note: For information on storing unused tofu, see page 7.

VEGETABLES

MOO SHU VEGETABLES

½ package dried black Chinese
mushrooms
(6 to 7 mushrooms)
2 tablespoons peanut or vegetable
oil
2 cloves garlic, minced
2 cups shredded napa cabbage or
green cabbage *or* preshredded
cabbage or coleslaw mix

1 red bell pepper, cut into short,
thin strips
1 cup fresh or rinsed, drained
canned bean sprouts
2 large green onions, cut into
short, thin strips
¼ cup hoisin sauce
⅓ cup plum sauce
8 flour tortillas (6 to 7 inches),
warmed

1. Place mushrooms in small bowl; cover with warm water. Soak 20 minutes to soften. Drain; squeeze out excess water. Discard stems; slice caps.

2. Heat wok or large skillet over medium-high heat. Add oil; heat until hot. Add garlic; stir-fry 30 seconds.

3. Add cabbage, mushrooms and red pepper; stir-fry 3 minutes. Add bean sprouts and onions; stir-fry 2 minutes. Add hoisin sauce; stir-fry 30 seconds or until mixture is hot.

4. Spread about 2 teaspoons plum sauce on each tortilla. Spoon heaping ¼ cup vegetable mixture over sauce. Fold bottom of tortilla up over filling, then fold sides over filling. *Makes 8 servings*

Note: For information on storing unused bean sprouts, see page 6.

SESAME-HONEY VEGETABLE CASSEROLE

1 package (16 ounces) frozen
mixed vegetable medley, such
as baby carrots, broccoli,
onions and red peppers,
thawed and drained

3 tablespoons honey
1 tablespoon Oriental sesame oil
1 tablespoon soy sauce
2 teaspoons sesame seeds

1. Preheat oven to 350°F. Place vegetables in shallow, 1½-quart casserole dish or quiche pan.

2. Combine remaining ingredients; mix well. Drizzle evenly over vegetables. Bake 20 to 25 minutes or until vegetables are hot, stirring after 15 minutes.

Makes 4 to 6 servings

DRAGON TOFU

To quickly cut squash, stack several slices, then cut into 2×¼-inch strips.

¼ cup soy sauce
1 tablespoon creamy peanut butter
1 package (about 12 ounces) firm tofu, drained
1 medium zucchini squash
1 medium yellow squash
2 teaspoons peanut or vegetable oil

½ teaspoon hot chili oil
2 cloves garlic, minced
2 cups packed fresh torn spinach leaves
¼ cup coarsely chopped cashews or peanuts (optional)

1. Whisk soy sauce into peanut butter in small bowl. Press tofu lightly between paper towels; cut into ¾-inch squares or triangles. Place in single layer in shallow dish. Pour soy sauce mixture over tofu; stir gently to coat all surfaces. Let stand at room temperature 20 minutes.

2. Cut zucchini and yellow squash into ¼-inch slices; cut each slice into 2×¼-inch strips.

3. Heat nonstick skillet over medium-high heat. Add peanut oil and chili oil; heat until hot. Add garlic and squash; stir-fry 3 minutes. Add tofu mixture; cook 2 minutes or until tofu is heated through and sauce is slightly thickened, stirring occasionally.

4. Stir in spinach; remove from heat. Sprinkle with cashews.

Makes 2 main-dish or 4 side-dish servings

SZECHUAN EGGPLANT

1 pound Oriental eggplants or regular eggplant, peeled
2 tablespoons peanut or vegetable oil
2 cloves garlic, minced
¼ teaspoon crushed red pepper flakes *or* ½ teaspoon hot chili oil

3 green onions, cut into 1-inch pieces
¼ cup hoisin sauce
¼ cup chicken broth
Toasted sesame seeds* (optional)

1. Cut eggplants into ½-inch slices; cut each slice into 2×½-inch strips.

2. Heat wok or large nonstick skillet over medium-high heat. Add peanut oil; heat until hot. Add eggplant, garlic and crushed red pepper; stir-fry 7 minutes or until eggplant is very tender and browned.

3. Reduce heat to medium. Add onions, hoisin sauce and broth; stir-fry 2 minutes. Sprinkle with sesame seeds.

Makes 4 to 6 servings

*To toast sesame seeds, spread seeds in small skillet. Shake skillet over medium heat 2 minutes or until seeds begin to pop and turn golden.

Dragon Tofu

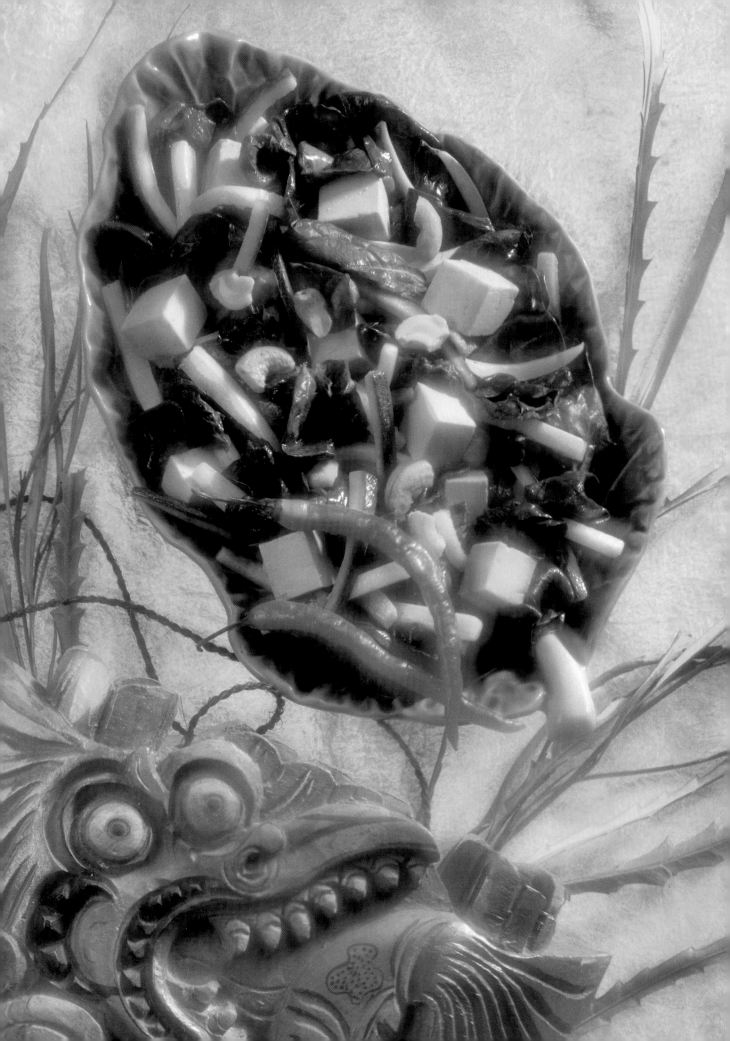

CHINESE SWEET AND SOUR VEGETABLES

3 cups broccoli florets
2 medium carrots, diagonally sliced
1 large red bell pepper, cut into short, thin strips
¼ cup water
2 teaspoons cornstarch
1 teaspoon sugar

⅓ cup unsweetened pineapple juice
1 tablespoon soy sauce
1 tablespoon rice vinegar
½ teaspoon Oriental sesame oil
¼ cup diagonally sliced green onions or chopped cilantro (optional)

1. Combine broccoli, carrots, and red pepper in large skillet with tight-fitting lid. Add water; bring to a boil over high heat. Reduce heat to medium. Cover and steam 4 minutes or until vegetables are crisp-tender.

2. Meanwhile, combine cornstarch and sugar in small bowl. Blend in pineapple juice, soy sauce and vinegar until smooth.

3. Transfer vegetables to colander; drain. Stir pineapple mixture and add to skillet. Cook and stir 2 minutes or until sauce boils and thickens.

4. Return vegetables to skillet; toss with sauce. Stir in sesame oil. Garnish with onions.
Makes 4 servings

THREE HAPPINESS MUSHROOMS

To save time, purchase pre-sliced fresh mushrooms and spinach leaves from the salad bar in your local supermarket.

1 package (1 ounce) dried black Chinese mushrooms
2 tablespoons peanut or vegetable oil
1 small yellow onion, cut into thin wedges
2 cloves garlic, minced

2 cups sliced fresh mushrooms
1 jar (7 ounces) straw mushrooms, drained
1 cup firmly packed fresh spinach leaves
3 tablespoons stir-fry sauce

1. Place dried mushrooms in small bowl; cover with warm water. Soak 20 minutes to soften. Drain; squeeze out excess water. Discard stems; slice caps.

2. Heat wok or large skillet over medium-high heat. Add oil; heat until hot. Add onion and garlic; stir-fry 6 minutes or until limp. Add dried, fresh and straw mushrooms; stir-fry 4 minutes.

3. Stir in spinach and stir-fry sauce; stir-fry 1 minute or until spinach is wilted and sauce is heated through.
Makes 4 servings

CASHEW GREEN BEANS

**1 package (10 ounces) frozen
  julienne-cut green beans,
  thawed and drained**
**1 tablespoon peanut or vegetable
  oil**
1 small onion, cut into thin wedges

2 cloves garlic, minced
2 tablespoons oyster sauce
1 tablespoon rice vinegar
1 tablespoon honey
**¼ cup coarsely chopped cashews
  or peanuts**

1. Pat green beans dry with paper towels.

2. Heat wok or large skillet over medium-high heat. Add oil; heat until hot. Add onion
and garlic; stir-fry 3 minutes.

3. Add beans; stir-fry 2 minutes. Add oyster sauce, vinegar and honey; stir-fry 1 minute
or until heated through. Remove from heat; stir in cashews.   *Makes 4 servings*

MONGOLIAN VEGETABLES

**1 package (about 12 ounces) firm
  tofu, drained**
4 tablespoons soy sauce, divided
1 tablespoon Oriental sesame oil
**1 large head bok choy (about
  1½ pounds)**
2 teaspoons cornstarch
**1 tablespoon peanut or vegetable
  oil**

**1 large red or yellow bell pepper,
  cut into short, thin strips**
2 cloves garlic, minced
**4 small *or* 2 large green onions,
  cut diagonally into ½-inch
  pieces**
2 teaspoons toasted sesame seeds*

1. Press tofu lightly between paper towels; cut into ¾-inch squares or triangles. Place
in shallow dish. Combine 2 tablespoons soy sauce and sesame oil; drizzle over tofu.
Let stand while preparing vegetables.

2. Cut woody stems from bok choy leaves; slice stems into ½-inch pieces. Cut tops of
leaves crosswise into ½-inch slices.

3. Blend remaining 2 tablespoons soy sauce into cornstarch in cup until smooth.

4. Heat wok or large skillet over medium-high heat. Add peanut oil; heat until hot.
Add bok choy stems, red pepper and garlic; stir-fry 5 minutes. Add onions and bok
choy leaves; stir-fry 2 minutes.

5. Stir soy sauce mixture and add to wok along with tofu mixture. Stir-fry 30 seconds
or until sauce boils and thickens. Sprinkle with sesame seeds.
           Makes 2 main-dish or 4 side-dish servings

*To toast sesame seeds, spread seeds in small skillet. Shake skillet over medium heat
2 minutes or until seeds begin to pop and turn golden.

BRAISED ORIENTAL CABBAGE

½ small head green cabbage (about
    ½ pound)
1 small head bok choy (about
    ¾ pound)
½ cup beef or chicken broth
2 tablespoons soy sauce

2 tablespoons rice vinegar
1 tablespoon brown sugar
¼ teaspoon crushed red pepper
    flakes (optional)
1 tablespoon water
1 tablespoon cornstarch

1. Cut cabbage into 1-inch pieces. Cut woody stems from bok choy leaves; slice stems into ½-inch pieces. Cut tops of leaves into ½-inch slices.

2. Combine cabbage and bok choy stems in 10-inch skillet. Add broth, soy sauce, vinegar, brown sugar and crushed red pepper.

3. Bring to a boil over high heat. Reduce heat to medium. Cover and simmer 5 minutes or until vegetables are crisp-tender.

4. Blend water into cornstarch in cup until smooth. Stir into skillet. Cook and stir 1 minute or until sauce boils and thickens.

5. Stir in reserved bok choy leaves; cook 1 minute more.   *Makes 4 to 6 servings*

HOT AND SOUR ZUCCHINI

2 teaspoons minced fresh ginger
1 clove garlic, minced
¼ teaspoon crushed red pepper
    flakes or crushed Szechuan
    peppercorns
1 pound zucchini
2 teaspoons sugar

1 teaspoon cornstarch
2 tablespoons red wine vinegar
2 tablespoons soy sauce
1 tablespoon peanut or vegetable
    oil
1 teaspoon Oriental sesame oil

1. Combine ginger, garlic and crushed red pepper in small bowl. Cut zucchini into ¼-inch slices. If zucchini is large, cut each slice in half. Toss zucchini with ginger mixture.

2. Combine sugar and cornstarch in small bowl. Blend in vinegar and soy sauce until smooth.

3. Heat large nonstick skillet over medium-high heat. Add peanut oil; heat until hot. Add zucchini mixture; stir-fry 4 to 5 minutes until zucchini is crisp-tender.

4. Stir vinegar mixture and add to skillet. Stir-fry 15 seconds or until sauce boils and thickens. Stir in sesame oil.   *Makes 4 servings*

ORANGE-ONION SALAD

The dressing for this simple salad gives it a fantastic flavor.

1 tablespoon soy sauce
1 tablespoon rice vinegar
2 teaspoons Oriental sesame oil
1 large navel orange, peeled and sliced

1 small red onion, thinly sliced
Romaine lettuce or spinach leaves
Carrot curls for garnish

1. Combine soy sauce, vinegar and sesame oil in small bowl.

2. Place orange and onion slices in single layer in shallow baking dish; drizzle with soy sauce mixture. Cover and refrigerate at least 30 minutes or up to 8 hours.

3. Transfer orange and onion slices to lettuce-lined serving platter or individual lettuce-lined dishes; drizzle with juices from dish. Garnish with carrot curls.

Makes 4 servings

ROASTED SHANGHAI PEPPER SALAD

Serve this salad as an accompaniment to grilled or broiled meats or fish.

1 jar (14 to 15 ounces) roasted red or red and yellow peppers
1½ tablespoons soy sauce
1 tablespoon rice vinegar
1 tablespoon Oriental sesame oil
2 teaspoons honey

1 clove garlic, minced
Romaine lettuce or spinach leaves
2 tablespoons coarsely chopped cilantro

1. Drain and rinse peppers; pat dry with paper towels. Cut peppers lengthwise into ½-inch strips; place in small bowl.

2. Combine soy sauce, vinegar, sesame oil, honey and garlic; mix well. Pour over peppers; cover and refrigerate at least 2 hours. Serve over lettuce leaves. Sprinkle with cilantro.

Makes 4 servings

Note: The salad will keep up to 1 week covered and refrigerated.

Top to bottom: Orange-Onion Salad and
Roasted Shanghai Pepper Salad

BUDDHA'S DELIGHT

1 package (1 ounce) dried black Chinese mushrooms
1 package (about 12 ounces) firm tofu, drained
1 tablespoon peanut or vegetable oil
2 cups diagonally cut 1-inch asparagus pieces *or* 1 package (10 ounces) frozen cut asparagus, thawed and drained

1 medium onion, cut into thin wedges
2 cloves garlic, minced
½ cup chicken broth
3 tablespoons hoisin sauce
¼ cup coarsely chopped cilantro or thinly sliced green onions

1. Place mushrooms in small bowl; cover with warm water. Soak 20 minutes to soften. Drain, squeezing out excess water over fine strainer into measuring cup; reserve. Discard mushroom stems; slice caps.

2. Press tofu lightly between paper towels; cut into ¾-inch squares or triangles.

3. Heat wok or large skillet over medium-high heat. Add oil; heat until hot. Add asparagus, onion wedges and garlic; stir-fry 4 minutes for fresh or 3 minutes for frozen asparagus.

4. Add mushrooms, ¼ cup reserved mushroom liquid,* broth and hoisin sauce. Reduce heat to medium-low. Simmer, uncovered, until asparagus is crisp-tender, 2 to 3 minutes for fresh or 1 minute for frozen asparagus.

5. Stir in tofu; heat through, stirring occasionally. Ladle into shallow bowls. Sprinkle with cilantro.   *Makes 2 main-dish or 4 side-dish servings*

*Remaining mushroom liquid may be covered and refrigerated up to 3 days or frozen up to 3 months. It may be used in soups and stews.

ORIENTAL SALAD SUPREME

¼ cup peanut or vegetable oil
¼ cup rice vinegar
2 tablespoons brown sugar
½ medium unpeeled cucumber, halved and sliced

6 cups torn romaine or leaf lettuce
1 cup chow mein noodles
¼ cup peanut halves or coarsely chopped cashews (optional)

1. Combine oil, vinegar and brown sugar in small bowl; whisk until sugar dissolves.* Toss with cucumbers. Marinate, covered, in the refrigerator up to 4 hours.

2. Just before serving, toss dressing with remaining ingredients.   *Makes 4 servings*

*At this point, dressing may be tossed with remaining ingredients and served immediately.

SZECHUAN-GRILLED MUSHROOMS

1 pound large fresh mushrooms
2 tablespoons soy sauce
2 teaspoons peanut or vegetable
  oil
1 teaspoon Oriental sesame oil

1 clove garlic, minced
½ teaspoon crushed Szechuan
  peppercorns or crushed red
  pepper flakes

1. Place mushrooms in large plastic bag. Add remaining ingredients to bag. Close bag securely; shake to coat mushrooms with marinade. Marinate at room temperature 15 minutes or cover and refrigerate up to 8 hours. (Mushrooms will absorb marinade.)

2. Thread mushrooms onto skewers. Grill or broil mushrooms 5 inches from heat 10 minutes or until lightly browned, turning once. Serve immediately.

Makes 4 servings

Variation: For *Szechuan-Grilled Mushrooms and Onions*, add 4 green onions, cut into 1½-inch pieces, to marinade. Alternately thread onto skewers with mushrooms. Proceed as directed in step 2.

STIR-FRIED SPINACH WITH GARLIC

2 teaspoons peanut or vegetable
  oil
1 large clove garlic, minced
6 cups packed fresh spinach
  leaves (about 8 ounces)

2 teaspoons soy sauce
1 teaspoon rice vinegar
¼ teaspoon sugar
1 teaspoon toasted sesame seeds*

1. Heat wok or large skillet over medium-high heat. Add oil; heat until hot. Add garlic; cook 1 minute.

2. Add spinach, soy sauce, vinegar and sugar; stir-fry 1 to 2 minutes until spinach is wilted. Sprinkle with sesame seeds.

Makes 2 servings

*To toast sesame seeds, spread seeds in small skillet. Shake skillet over medium heat 2 minutes or until seeds begin to pop and turn golden.

MARINATED CUCUMBERS

Serve as a salad or a condiment with pork or chicken dishes.

1 large cucumber (about
  12 ounces)
2 tablespoons rice vinegar
2 tablespoons peanut or vegetable
  oil

2 tablespoons soy sauce
1½ teaspoons sugar
1 clove garlic, minced
¼ teaspoon crushed red pepper
  flakes

1. Score cucumber lengthwise with tines of fork. Cut in half lengthwise; scrape out and discard seeds. Cut crosswise into ⅛-inch slices; place in medium bowl.

2. Combine remaining ingredients in cup; pour over cucumber. Toss to coat. Cover and refrigerate at least 4 hours or up to 2 days.

Makes 4 to 6 servings

MA PO TOFU

This lighter version of a Szechuan specialty omits the pork and adds vegetables.

1 package (about 12 ounces) firm
    tofu, drained
2 tablespoons soy sauce
2 teaspoons minced fresh ginger
1 cup chicken broth, divided
1 tablespoon cornstarch

1½ cups broccoli florets
1 teaspoon hot chili oil
2 teaspoons Oriental sesame oil
¼ cup coarsely chopped cilantro or
    green onion tops

1. Press tofu lightly between paper towels; cut into ¾-inch squares or triangles. Place in shallow dish; sprinkle with soy sauce and ginger.

2. Blend ¼ cup broth into cornstarch in cup until smooth. Combine remaining ¾ cup broth, broccoli and chili oil in 10-inch skillet. Bring to a boil over high heat. Reduce heat to medium. Cover and cook 3 minutes or until broccoli is crisp-tender.

3. Stir broth mixture and add to skillet. Cook and stir 1 minute or until sauce boils and thickens. Stir in tofu mixture. Simmer, uncovered, until tofu is hot. Stir in sesame oil. Sprinkle with cilantro. *Makes 2 main-dish or 4 side-dish servings*

ROASTED VEGETABLES WITH NOODLES

Oven roasting gives these vegetables a browned appearance.

5 tablespoons soy sauce, divided
3 tablespoons peanut or vegetable
    oil
2 tablespoons rice vinegar
2 cloves garlic, minced
½ pound large fresh mushrooms
4 ounces shallots
1 medium zucchini squash, cut
    into 1-inch pieces, each cut
    into halves
1 medium yellow crookneck
    squash, cut into 1-inch pieces,
    each cut into halves

1 red bell pepper, cut into 1-inch
    pieces
1 yellow bell pepper, cut into
    1-inch pieces
2 small Oriental eggplants, cut
    into ½-inch slices *or* 2 cups
    cubed eggplant
8 ounces Chinese egg noodles or
    vermicelli, hot cooked,
    drained
1 tablespoon Oriental sesame oil
1 teaspoon sugar

1. Preheat oven to 425°F. Combine 2 tablespoons soy sauce, peanut oil, vinegar and garlic in small bowl; mix well.

2. Combine vegetables in shallow roasting pan (do not line pan with foil). Toss with soy sauce mixture to coat well.

3. Roast vegetables 20 minutes or until browned and tender, stirring well after 10 minutes.

4. Place noodles in large bowl. Toss hot noodles with remaining 3 tablespoons soy sauce and sesame oil.

5. Toss roasted vegetables with noodle mixture; serve warm or at room temperature.
Makes 6 servings

INDEX

Almond Chicken, 42
Appetizers
Barbecued Ribs, 24
Chilled Shrimp in Chinese Mustard Sauce, 15
Chinatown Stuffed Mushrooms, 11
Crab Cakes Canton, 21
Easy Wonton Chips, 10
Egg Rolls, 15
Marinated Vegetables, 16
Mini-Marinated Beef Skewers, 16
Oriental Chicken Wings, 11
Oriental Salsa, 14
Shrimp Toast, 18
Spicy Beef Turnovers, 20
Spicy Chicken Bundles, 12
Spring Rolls, 12
Asparagus and Ham, Shanghai Chicken with, 46

Barbecued Ribs, 24
Bean Threads with Tofu and Vegetables, 79
Beef
Beef and Broccoli, 32
Beef Soup with Noodles, 10
Beef with Bean Threads and Cabbage, 24
Beef with Leeks and Tofu, 38
Beef with Oyster Sauce, 35
Egg Rolls, 15
Fragrant Beef with Garlic Sauce, 26
Ginger Beef, 34
Meat Patties with Chinese Gravy, 36
Ming Dynasty Beef Stew, 29
Mini-Marinated Beef Skewers, 16
Mongolian Hot Pot, 28
Orange Beef, 28
Oriental Beef with Vegetables, 41
Pepper Beef, 22
Sesame-Garlic Flank Steak, 40
Spicy Beef Turnovers, 20
Spicy Beef with Noodles, 30
Beijing Fillet of Sole, 66
Braised Oriental Cabbage, 87
Broccoli, Beef and, 32
Broiled Hunan Fish Fillets, 69
Buddha's Delight, 90

Cabbage
Beef with Bean Threads and Cabbage, 24
Braised Oriental Cabbage, 87
Cantonese Rice Cake Patties, 74
Canton Pork Stew, 36
Cashew Chicken, 59
Cashew Green Beans, 86
Cellophane Noodle Salad, 72
Chicken (*see also* **Cornish Hens**)
Almond Chicken, 42
Cashew Chicken, 59
Chicken and Corn Soup, 18
Chicken Chop Suey, 54
Chicken Chow Mein, 56
Chinese Chicken Salad, 50
Chinese Chicken Stew, 52
Chinese Curried Chicken, 58
Cilantro-Stuffed Chicken Breasts, 50
Crispy Roasted Chicken, 46
Garlicky Baked Chicken, 52
Gingered Chicken Thighs, 44
Hoisin-Roasted Chicken with Vegetables, 56
Honey-Lime Glazed Chicken, 48
Kung Po Chicken, 59
Moo Goo Gai Pan, 48
Oriental Chicken Kabobs, 49
Oriental Chicken Wings, 11
Sesame Chicken, 58
Shanghai Chicken with Asparagus and Ham, 46
Spicy Chicken Bundles, 12
Szechuan Chicken Salad with Peanut Dressing, 49
Chilled Shrimp in Chinese Mustard Sauce, 15
Chinatown Stuffed Mushrooms, 11
Chinese Barbecued Pork, 41
Chinese Chicken Salad, 50
Chinese Chicken Stew, 52
Chinese Curried Chicken, 58
Chinese Sweet and Sour Vegetables, 84
Cilantro-Stuffed Chicken Breasts, 50
Cornish Hens
Orange-Ginger Broiled Cornish Hens, 54
Pineapple-Hoisin Hens, 44
Corn Soup, Chicken and, 18
Crab Cakes Canton, 21
Crispy Roasted Chicken, 46
Cucumbers, Marinated, 92
Curried Noodles, 79

Dragon Tofu, 82

Easy Seafood Stir-Fry, 60
Easy Wonton Chips, 10
Egg Drop Soup, 20
Egg Foo Yung, 78
Egg Noodles with Oyster Sauce and Green Onions, 74
Eggplant, Szechuan, 82
Egg Rolls, 15
Eggs
Egg Drop Soup, 20
Egg Foo Yung, 78
Ginger Noodles with Sesame Egg Strips, 75